Teaching English Pronunciation for a Global World

Teaching English Pronunciation for a Global World

Robin Walker and Gemma Archer

OXFORD
UNIVERSITY PRESS

Great Clarendon Street, Oxford, OX2 6DP, United Kingdom

Oxford University Press is a department of the University of Oxford.
It furthers the University's objective of excellence in research, scholarship,
and education by publishing worldwide. Oxford is a registered trade
mark of Oxford University Press in the UK and in certain other countries

ISBN: 978 0 19 408898 5

Printed in China

This book is printed on paper from certified and well-managed sources

ACKNOWLEDGEMENTS

*The authors and publisher are grateful to those who have given permission
to reproduce the following extracts and adaptations of copyright material*:
p.67 Figure 'Pronunciation Journey' by Mark Hancock, © Mark Hancock.
Reproduced by permission; p.42 Extract from English File 4th Edition
Elementary Student Book by Christina Latham-Koenig, Clive Oxenden
and Jerry Lambert, with Paul Seligson, © Oxford University Press 2019.
Reproduced by permission.

Illustrations: QBS Learning

Front cover photo: Shutterstock/CarlosBarquero

*Although every effort has been made to trace and contact copyright holders
before publication, this has not been possible in some cases. We apologise for any
apparent infringement of copyright and, if notified, the publisher will be pleased to
rectify any errors or omissions at the earliest possible opportunity.*

Acknowledgements

The ideas in this book and the principles behind them all stem from the pioneering work of Jennifer Jenkins on the pronunciation of English as an international language. Jenkins' work was stimulated in part by Bryan Jenner's earlier ideas on intelligibility and a common core of teaching priorities. Both Jenner and Jenkins published ground-breaking articles about their work in *Speak Out!*, the journal of the IATEFL Pronunciation Special Interest Group (PronSIG). Our discussions over the years with members of the PronSIG have been fundamental in shaping and fine-tuning the ideas in this book. In that respect, we are especially grateful to Adam Scott for his generous contributions to the early stages of the book's creation. Last, but not at all least, we would like to thank the hundreds of students and teachers who have taken part in courses, workshops, webinars, and training sessions on the pronunciation of English. We have been stimulated and motivated every step of the way by their interest, enthusiasm, and energy.

Contents

Introduction

We live in a world of constant change. The way we relate to each other through social media, for example, was unimaginable only ten years ago, and ten years from now it will be different again. In response to this ever-changing world, languages themselves are constantly evolving. They do this so that their users can interact meaningfully with the world in which they live. All languages do this, and in that respect, English is no different from any other language. But what marks English out as different is the question of who is driving the change.

Language change is brought about by its users. For most languages, the users are predominantly its native speakers. But in the case of English, there are more than four times as many non-native speakers as there are native speakers. By using English in their daily lives, non-native speakers are bringing about unexpected changes. Increasingly, non-native speakers use English as a neutral, shared language for international communication. This communication often takes place in the absence of native speakers, and so is referred to as **English as a lingua franca (ELF)**, or as **English as an international language (EIL)**. The terms are similar but not identical, but the differences between them do not concern us here. In this book, we will use the term EIL. What does concern us here, however, is that both ELF and EIL differ in significant ways from the English that native speakers use among themselves. This is the variety normally taught in classes of **English as a foreign language (EFL)**, or in classes for immigrants in countries like the UK, the US, Australia, or New Zealand.

The fact that the same language can be used in different ways by different users should not surprise us. If you are not a native speaker, you may have observed that in order to communicate efficiently with fellow non-native speakers, you sometimes use English in ways that a native speaker wouldn't. These new ways of using English are often in the use of vocabulary and idiomatic language. However, the area where English as an international language differs most markedly from what we typically teach in an EFL setting is pronunciation, which is the subject of this book. More than vocabulary, and far more than grammar, pronunciation is the area of English language teaching that requires us as teachers to rethink our classroom practice if we aspire to equip our learners for today's (and tomorrow's) world.

Who the book is for

Do you teach English to students who are likely to use their English for international communication in the future, or who are already doing so?

This is the case, for example, throughout Europe, Asia, Southeast Asia, South America, the Middle East, and the Mediterranean basin. Are you teaching young learners, teenagers, or adults? Are you aware of the role of English as an international language, but unsure as to what that means in terms of teaching pronunciation? Are you interested in the pronunciation of English but unsure as to how to teach it in class? If you have answered 'yes' to any of these questions, this book is for you. And even if your job is to teach pronunciation with the aim of getting your students to sound like native speakers, most of the activities in this book, and one whole chapter, will be of use to you, too.

What's in the book

There are ten chapters in this book, and these are grouped into three sections. The first is about learner goals and teaching priorities. Without these, learners are unlikely to be motivated, and teaching is unlikely to be effective. The second section of the book is about teaching the pronunciation of consonants, vowels, **word stress**, and **sentence stress**, since these are the areas of pronunciation that, according to research, have most impact on a speaker's **intelligibility** in EIL use of English. You should work through these first four chapters before you go on to the other six. The last, and longest, section is about teaching techniques, including topics such as how we can use technology in our teaching of pronunciation, how we can harness the learner's mother tongue, and how we can assess the progress our students have made. These six chapters can be dipped into in any order.

Some words of advice

Firstly, this book cannot offer you all of the activities that you can use to teach the pronunciation of EIL. So do not be afraid to use activities you are already familiar with, provided they are consistent with the goal of **international intelligibility**. Chapter 1 and Appendix 1 will help you to select appropriate activities from those you already regularly use.

Secondly, remember that no two teaching situations are the same. You could be teaching in a country where English is the first language for the vast majority of the population, as is the case for one of the authors, or you could be teaching in a country where English is rarely spoken outside the classroom, and where the students share a common first language. This is the situation in which the second author has worked for over forty years. But whatever your teaching situation, remember that you are the person who knows best what your students need; you are the one to best understand which of the activities in this book to use and which to ignore, which to use as described, and which to adapt.

Part 1   Goals and priorities

1 Goals and priorities

Goals are essential to teaching, and this is as true for pronunciation as it is for every other aspect of learning English. Meaningful goals motivate us and give direction to the work we do, as well as providing a sense of achievement when one goal is achieved and a new one set. Setting priorities is also essential when teaching pronunciation, partly because of the limited time we have in class with our students, but also because the goal we have set influences the way we prioritize.

For a long time, the goal of pronunciation teaching was widely seen as achieving, as closely as possible, a native-speaker **accent**. The arrival of communicative approaches in the 1980s, however, caused some pronunciation experts to a call for a change. They argued that it was not necessary to strive to sound like a native speaker; rather, it was enough for learners' pronunciation to be comfortably intelligible.

Not everyone took to the new goal wholeheartedly, but today, major international exam boards and institutions like the Council of Europe see intelligibility as a much more relevant goal than a native-speaker accent. In the 2018 update to the Common European Framework of Reference, for example, the Council of Europe openly states that its original focus on native-speaker accents was mistaken, and that it is more appropriate to focus on intelligibility when assessing a learner's pronunciation as good or not.

This shift from the goal of a native-speaker accent to one of intelligibility is welcome, but it is still problematic. In the minds of many ELT professionals, consciously or otherwise, the listener who should judge if a learner's pronunciation is or is not intelligible is invariably a native speaker of English. And this is where the problem lies since, as we saw in the introduction, there are far more non-native speakers of English than native speakers. And, when two or more non-native speakers come together through English, they are the ones who should judge what is intelligible and what is not.

The goal of all learners is good pronunciation, and helping learners to achieve this is the driving force behind the activities in this book. However, good pronunciation can no longer be defined in terms of a single accent. Rather, it is the ability of the speaker to pronounce sounds in a way that is comfortably intelligible to the listener, regardless of the speaker's accent, and regardless of the listener's first language. This exciting new goal brings with it new, highly attainable teaching priorities.

Raising awareness about accent and intelligibility

It is not enough for us as teachers to understand the reasoning behind international intelligibility as the principal goal of pronunciation teaching today; our students also need to see the value of this new goal. The activities in this chapter, which are best suited to classes of upper-secondary or adult learners, are designed to help them do that. It is important that these older students see the benefits of aiming for international intelligibility. A poor understanding of this goal is likely to affect their motivation, and as a result, reduce the impact of the pronunciation activities you do.

On the other hand, these awareness-raising activities are not appropriate for young and very young learners. As their teacher, you need to continue to make decisions regarding their pronunciation goals on their behalf, just as you have done up to now. In a limited number of situations, that might mean continuing to work towards the goal of a native-speaker accent. In most cases, however, the goal of international intelligibility will be a better choice. This is especially true where young learners, while growing up, are most likely to use their English with other non-native speakers.

Try this    **How good is your pronunciation?**

Give your students the chance to explore some of the issues involved in aiming for native-speaker or non-native-speaker accents.

- Give each student a copy of the 'Good pronunciation' quiz on page 14. Allow them time to read it and to choose their answers.
- Put the students in pairs to compare their answers. Encourage them to explain to each other why they made the choices they did.
- In large classes, bring pairs of students together to make groups of four. Again, encourage students to compare their answers and justify their choices. With small classes, invite them to get up and walk around the room talking to as many classmates as they can. While they are discussing their answers, go around the room and listen in to their discussions.
- Bring the class together and go through the questions in a whole-class discussion.

✓ *Getting it right*   During the early phases, avoid suggesting that there might be correct or incorrect answers. Then, during the class discussion, rather than say that certain answers are correct, ask for a show of hands to gauge what the class feels about each point. Next, ask individual students to explain their choices. Finally, use the discussion points below to tell them what is known about each point.

Good pronunciation quiz

Circle the option or options that you think are correct.

1 **The most common English accent in the world is:**

   a) Australian English b) American English c) British English d) Indian English e) non-native-speaker English.

2 **The most easily understood English accent in the world is:**

   a) Australian English b) American English c) British English d) Indian English e) non-native-speaker English.

3 **The percentage of problems of intelligibility in English that are the result of poor pronunciation is:**

   a) 0% b) 4% c) 28% d) 63% e) 85%.

4 **Most of these problems of intelligibility are due to the poor pronunciation of:**

   a) consonant sounds b) rhythm and intonation c) sentence stress d) word stress e) vowel sounds.

5 **Good English pronunciation is:**

   a) as close to a British English accent as possible b) as close to an American English accent as you can get c) as close to any native-speaker accent as you can get d) easily intelligible to whoever you are talking to e) easily intelligible to your classmates.

Good pronunciation quiz: discussion of points

1   The answer is e). There are far more speakers of American English than of Australian or British English, but 2021 estimates calculate 125 million first-language speakers of English in India, making it second only to the US, which has around 310 million. The UK has around 58 million first-language speakers of English according to a 2021 government census, and worldwide, a generally accepted figure for native speakers of English is 373 million. Similar calculations estimate that there are at least 1,100 million non-native speakers who are competent users of English in the world today. This means that English is spoken by many more non-native speakers – with all of their many and varied accents.

2   There is no single correct answer. The most easily understood accent is the one a listener is used to hearing. Because teaching materials often employ a standard native-speaker accent, learners inevitably find the accent from their coursebooks easier to understand than other accents. However, a native-speaker accent is not automatically more intelligible than a non-native-speaker accent. Non-native speakers who use English for international communication outside the classroom environment regularly report that they find other non-native speakers easier to understand than native speakers.

3   The answer is d). Research done in the late 1990s found that for B2- to C1-level speakers of English, pronunciation lay behind over 60% of the breakdowns in spoken communication in English between non-native speakers. Later research more or less confirmed this. Problems with

grammar, on the other hand, only accounted for 4% of breakdowns in communication, with vocabulary being the cause of about 30% of misunderstandings. This strongly suggests a pivotal role for pronunciation in international spoken communication in English.

4 There is no single correct answer. The same research as that referred to in answer 3 found that consonant sounds and sentence stress are central to international intelligibility, while rhythm and intonation were not found to have any significant impact, either positive or negative. With vowels, differences in length were found to be far more important than exact qualities or 'regional flavours' (see Chapter 3). There is still no conclusive research as to the importance of word stress for international intelligibility.

5 Here the clear answer is d). Even if you are a native speaker, your aim should be to make yourself understood by your listener or listeners. And the most competent speakers can modify their pronunciation to help any listener who is struggling to understand them.

 **Getting it right**

An alternative to leading a class discussion using the information above is to photocopy the information and give one discussion point to each student in a group of five. The students study their information point and then explain it to the rest of their group in their own words. Monitor their discussions and help with anything they don't understand.

Why this works ▐▐▶

We know from experience that if we do not have control over something that we are required to do, we are not strongly motivated to do it. This activity helps students to see why international intelligibility is a meaningful alternative goal to a native-speaker accent. In combination with the other activities in this chapter, this one should help learners to begin to shift their attention away from native-speaker accents and towards being internationally intelligible.

Try this ☞ **What's in it for us?**

Even if you introduce the goal of international intelligibility carefully with activities such as the previous one, it is quite natural for students to be reluctant to accept it at first. A discussion of the possible advantages and disadvantages of the new approach can be a productive way of getting them to explore their concerns.

- Put the students into small groups. Invite them to share any worries or concerns they have about adopting international intelligibility as their goal as opposed to a native-speaker accent.
- Invite a group to tell the class one of their concerns. Put a note about it on the class board. If necessary, prompt the class: 'Is anyone concerned that they might fail an exam because they don't have a native-speaker accent?'

 **Getting it right**

Don't expect too many answers at this stage. You might even be met by an uncomfortable silence. This is quite normal: your students won't have thought about goals for their pronunciation very much until now, if at all.

- Give each group a copy of Table 1.1 and invite the students to work together to decide which statements are true and which are false.

- When the groups have made their decisions, invite them to share their answers with the rest of the class, and to explain their thinking behind each answer.
- Round off any discussion about each statement by introducing the ideas summarized in the comments below.

 **Getting it right**

In classes where the students and teacher share the same mother tongue, it is quite natural for students to get so engaged in their discussions that they start to use their shared first language. If this allows them to explore some of the complexities of the points under discussion more freely, then it should be encouraged.

Statements	True	False	Reasons / thoughts
1) A non-native-speaker accent makes a bad impression.			
2) A speaker who is Japanese or Egyptian can sound as if they are from Japan or Egypt and still be completely intelligible.			
3) If learners don't try to sound like a native speaker, they won't have a model to imitate when practising pronunciation.			
4) It is easier to learn to be internationally intelligible than to learn to speak English with a native-speaker accent.			
5) Teachers don't need to be native speakers in order to teach the pronunciation of international intelligibility well.			
6) The speaking part of international English language exams judges pronunciation on its nearness to a near-native-speaker accent.			

TABLE I.I. *Prompts for a discussion about the advantages and disadvantages of aiming for international intelligibility*

Comments
1. False. A small number of users of English, mostly native speakers, will judge a speaker negatively because of their non-native-speaker accent. But the vast majority of English speakers today will judge a person by how intelligible they are. In addition, there are some speakers of English who enjoy hearing different accents, regardless of whether these are native or non-native.
2. True. As with Statement 1, the key is that a speaker needs to be intelligible. But if you are a guide showing tourists Mount Fuji or the Pyramids, then sounding Japanese or Egyptian will allow people to see that you are a native of that country, something that will usually be seen as a positive attribute.
3. False. If your learners aim at international intelligibility, they can imitate anybody they know who is already internationally intelligible. This could be you, their teacher, a good friend, or a celebrity who regularly uses English for international communication.

4. True. The workload required to achieve international intelligibility is significantly lighter and is more easily achieved than the workload for a learner who wants to sound like a native speaker.

5. True. Traditionally, native speakers have been seen as best at teaching pronunciation, but this is not the case when the goal is intelligibility. In fact, in some ways, non-native-speaking teachers can be better. They have personal experience at learning to do what they are asking their students to do, and they often have very good knowledge of the students' first-language phonology and any problems it might present.

6. False. None of the major EFL exam boards (Cambridge, Trinity College London, TOEFL, etc.) use proximity to a native-speaker accent in their marking criteria for pronunciation. In all cases, pronunciation is referenced to intelligibility and ease of understanding.

Why this works ▶

The idea of international intelligibility as their pronunciation goal will be new to many students, and this will generate concerns as to whether or not they are going in the right direction. This type of activity can help your students see that not only are some of their fears unfounded (Statements 1, 3, and 6), but that there are clear benefits to be gained by making international intelligibility their goal (Statements 2 and 5).

Try this ☞ **I want to sound like them!**

One of the most powerful arguments for aiming to be internationally intelligible is the number of successful people around the world who are not native speakers of English: CEOs of major companies, top sportspeople, or film or music celebrities. The key point here is that there are many highly successful people whose accents are not native, but who are clearly intelligible when they use English in their professional lives.

• Ask your students to tell you the names of internationally successful people whom they admire, and who regularly use English for international communication. Write the names that they come up with on the class board.

 **Getting it right**

Teenagers will most probably bring up the names of pop musicians and singers, or men and women from the world of sport, like football or tennis. Adults are more likely to suggest the names of film stars or successful business people. The key is for your students to make the choices themselves. It is also a good idea to encourage them to suggest both people who share your students' first language, and those from other first-language backgrounds.

• Get the students to talk to the class about the personality they have proposed – what they do, why they use English, how fluent they seem to be, if they sound like a native speaker, etc.

• Put the students into pairs, and ask each pair to choose one of the international personalities whose name has come up in class. Tell them to try to find a short video of their personality speaking English and to send you the link to the video, as well as bookmarking the link on their phones.

• In the next class, team up two or three pairs and get them to share their videos. Invite them to comment on how well their personality speaks English.

- Show the class one or two videos from the links you were sent. Include both very fluent and less fluent speakers, but also highly intelligible and less intelligible speakers.
- End with a whole-class discussion. Get this going by asking your students questions like: 'Do you get the impression that these people are embarrassed because they don't sound like native speakers?', 'Do you think that their non-native-speaker accents have been an obstacle on their road to success?', 'Which do you think they would want if they had to choose: to sound like a native speaker or to be successful at their sport/profession?'

Why this works ▥▶ This activity helps students to see that having a non-native-speaker accent in English is clearly not an obstacle to being successful in a wide range of activities and professions that require English for professional communication. In short, highly successful non-native-speaking professionals are great models for students in terms of their English pronunciation.

Try this ☞ **What matters most**

Students can achieve a high level of international intelligibility if they concentrate their efforts on four or five aspects of the pronunciation of English. However, rather than tell them what these are, let them try to guess.

- Put the students into pairs or small groups. Give them a copy of Table 1.2, which details the main aspects of pronunciation.

 **Getting it right** Be ready to explain what the terms in Column 1 mean, and to provide clear examples of each aspect of pronunciation, preferably using pronunciation exercises from your students' coursebook.

- Ask them to think about the goal of achieving a native-speaker accent, and the alternative goal of international intelligibility.
- Tell the pairs/groups to decide which of these aspects are VIP (= very important), IP (= important), or NIP (= not important) in order to achieve each of the different goals. This has been done for sentence stress as an example.

Aspects of English pronunciation	Native-speaker accent	International intelligibility
1. Consonants		
2. Vowels		
3. Word stress		
4. Sentence stress	VIP	VIP
5. Weak form words		
6. Rhythm		
7. Intonation		

TABLE I.2　*The main aspects of pronunciation*

- When the students have had time to complete both columns of the table, get them to focus their attention on the goal of a native-speaker accent. Ask them to say which aspect(s) are VIP, like sentence stress, which are IP, and which are NIP.

- Allow a discussion to develop naturally as to the VIP/IP/NIP options, and invite students to explain their choices. Finally, reveal to the class that in order to achieve a native-speaker accent, every one of the seven aspects is VIP. Insist that any deviation in any of the aspects means you will not sound like a native.
- Now invite the class to suggest which aspects are VIP for the goal of international intelligibility. Again, encourage the students to explain their choices.
- Tell your students that research strongly suggests that the VIP areas for international intelligibility are:
  - ♦ consonants
  - ♦ sentence stress
  - ♦ the long–short aspect of English vowels. Here you will need to explain that the quality or 'flavour' of English vowels (i.e. *bus* being pronounced as /bʌs/ or /bus/) is the main difference between different accents, but that this is not critical for international intelligibility.
- Finish by explaining that:
  - ♦ word stress might be important or might not, but until more research has been done, you are going to include it in your list
  - ♦ rhythm and intonation are not important
  - ♦ **weak forms** of words are not important, and can even be damaging to international intelligibility. This is because they can reduce some syllables to the point where they are inaudible, and that can make it very hard to recognize words in the speech flow.

Why this works ▌▌▌➡ One of the most convincing arguments in favour of an international intelligibility approach to teaching English is that the number of key aspects of pronunciation is smaller and more achievable than what is required for a native-speaker accent. Once it has been correctly completed, the table in this activity can be displayed in the classroom as a powerful reminder of the priorities for learners aiming at being internationally intelligible, and of the much greater workload for those aiming for a native-speaker accent. Chapters 2, 3, and 4 introduce activities aimed at developing your students' competence in the priority areas for international intelligibility. Together, these areas are known as the **Lingua Franca Core (LFC)**. Full details of the LFC can be found in Appendix 1.

Part 2   Towards intelligibility

2   Consonants

For many teachers, pronunciation practice is something they know they should do more of, but they are often unsure where to start or what is most important. Research shows us that time spent working on consonant sounds is well spent, as consonants play a vital role in making English intelligible for an international audience.

What is a consonant sound?

A consonant sound is made when we use our **articulators**, that is, our tongue, lips, jaw, and teeth, to obstruct and shape the airflow as it leaves the body through the mouth (see Figure 2.1). Unlike in vowel sounds, the process of pronouncing a consonant is usually very visible, making it easier for us to see and describe to students, which in turn can help us to guide their practice and production.

The articulators

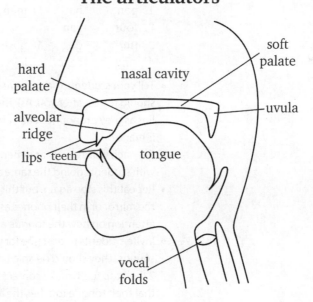

FIGURE 2.1.   *The articulators*

Try this ☞   **Exploiting the visual nature of consonants**

In this activity, students discover some of the different parts of the mouth involved in producing consonant sounds. They will observe you as you lead them through the exercise, as well as feel and observe their own pronunciation using one of the following tools:

- a hand mirror, or a mobile phone in selfie mode: these will enable students to see the inside of their mouths as they move their articulators and produce consonant sounds.
- a poster or image of the inside of the mouth which can be projected onto a whiteboard or screen. This will enable you to point to where a sound is being produced and name the articulators such as the tongue, lips, or teeth. There are many images of the mouth available online, such as the one in Figure 2.2.

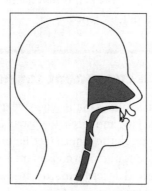

FIGURE 2.2.   *The inside of the mouth*

- Write four groups of words on the board, underlining the consonants as follows:
  1. <u>p</u>en   <u>b</u>at   <u>m</u>an
  2. <u>f</u>our   <u>v</u>an
  3. <u>t</u>ie   <u>d</u>og   <u>n</u>ose   <u>l</u>ip
  4. ri<u>ng</u>   ca<u>k</u>e   lo<u>g</u>

- Tell your students that you are going to say each word aloud, line by line, and they should repeat after you. Ask them to focus all their attention on their tongue and lips as they pronounce each underlined sound. What do they do when each sound is made?
- Say each word aloud, and then pronounce its underlined consonant in isolation, with students doing the same after you. For example: pen /p/, bat /b/, man /m/.
- Repeat this step again, but this time ask students to look at their mouths in the mirror or in their phones as they say the underlined sounds, focusing their attention on how the tongue and lips move.
- Invite students to describe for you what they see as they say these underlined sounds. They should be able to see that in line 1 their lips come together; in line 2 their top teeth make contact with their lower lip; in line 3 they might see or feel that their tongue touches the area behind their top teeth; and in line 4 the tongue moves to the back of the mouth.
- Demonstrate lip position and movement to clarify or correct students' answers for lines 1 and 2. For lines 3 and 4, refer to an image of the mouth, such as the one in Figure 2.2, to point out where the tongue is, what it's touching or where it moves to.

✓ Getting it right This activity is very flexible: it can be used as described above, or it can be used a little at a time to focus on specific sounds or provide corrections. However, if you decide to use an image such as that in Figure 2.2, or even a video, it is important to first provide students with a short explanation of what they are seeing. If they have never seen an image showing the inside of the mouth before, they may not fully understand what they are looking at. A brief explanation at the beginning will remove this distraction and reduce any confusion.

Voicing

A key feature of consonant sounds is **voicing**, created by the vibration of the vocal cords during the pronunciation of a sound. While most English consonants are voiced, some are not. These **unvoiced** sounds rely instead on the articulators, as described above, for their pronunciation. As not all languages have the same distribution of voiced and unvoiced consonants, making students aware of this difference is important. Mixing up voiced and unvoiced consonants can change the meaning of the words, as shown in Table 2.1, thereby affecting intelligibility.

Voiced consonant sounds	Unvoiced consonant sound equivalent
/b/ bat	/p/ pat
/d/ down	/t/ town
/g/ guard	/k/ card
/v/ vest	/f/ for
/ð/ breathe	/θ/ breath
/z/ zip	/s/ sip
/ʒ/ vision	/ʃ/ fish
/dʒ/ joke	/tʃ/ choke
/r/ red	
/l/ long	
/n/ now	
/m/ may	
/ŋ/ talking	
/w/ want	

TABLE 2.1. *The voiced and unvoiced consonant sounds of English*

Try this ☞ **Introducing voicing to students**

- Pronounce the unvoiced /s/ sound, making it as long as you can without stopping for breath.
- Repeat this sound, inviting your students to copy you. After a few seconds, put your hand over your throat. Encourage your students to do the same.

- Now repeat the process, but halfway through, begin voicing the sound, turning /s/ to /z/. Gesture with your hands to draw students' attention to the change of sound and encourage them to begin voicing, with their hand still in place over their throat.
- Once you have finished making the two sounds, ask the students if they were the same or different 'here', pointing to your throat. They should have felt a difference between the two sounds.

✔ *Getting it right*

This activity, where you demonstrate turning the vocal cords 'on and off' in just one breath, will only work with fricative sounds where your long continuous breath can escape through a small narrow passage and out through the mouth. As such, the voiced and unvoiced pairs /s/ and /z/, /f/ and /v/, /θ/ and /ð/, and /ʃ/ and /ʒ/ can easily be demonstrated in this way, but not other consonant pairs like /p/ and /b/, /t/ and /d/, or /k/ and /g/.

Try this ☞   **Hearing and making voiced and unvoiced consonants**

Once you have shown students the difference between voiced and unvoiced sounds, the following activity will provide them with time to practise distinguishing between them, and then producing them. This can begin in a controlled style at first, with you leading the activity, but once you feel students have understood, allow them to practise with a partner.

- Prepare a list of **minimal pairs**, in which the only sound which differs is the voiced or unvoiced consonant. Refer to Table 2.1 for ideas on the types of words you can use for this, or locate examples by observing your students' own speech. Your list could look something like that shown in Figure 2.3:

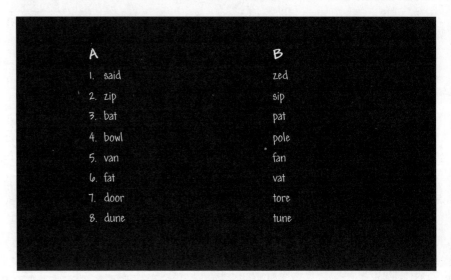

	A	B
1.	said	zed
2.	zip	sip
3.	bat	pat
4.	bowl	pole
5.	van	fan
6.	fat	vat
7.	door	tore
8.	dune	tune

FIGURE 2.3.   *Sample words for distinguishing between voiced and unvoiced consonants*

- Write your list on the board in two columns: A and B.
- Tell students you will say only one word from each pair. They must listen carefully and tell you if they heard the word in column A or B. You can ask students to shout out their answer, or invite them individually to contribute answers.

- Work through the list. If anyone volunteers the incorrect answer, invite them to put their hand on their throat and say the word for themselves to see if the voicing (or lack of it) helps them to self-correct.
- When you have finished, arrange the students into pairs. Ask them to secretly choose one word from each pair to say aloud to their partner. Then, one student says their pre-selected list of words, and the other listens and identifies which words they have heard. They then swap roles.
- Monitor the students as they complete this exercise, reminding them to ask for repetition if their partner's pronunciation is not clear, and to put their hand on their throat if that helps them to say the word correctly.

 **Getting it right**

When selecting minimal pairs for this activity, choose only those that have the voiced or unvoiced sound at the beginning of the word. Voicing of word-final consonants is either very weak or is not there at all. See the section on vowel length in Chapter 3 for more details of this phenomenon.

Why this works ▐▐▐▶

This simple exercise raises students' awareness of the difference between voiced and unvoiced sounds, and provides them with a means of checking their own production. The gesture of the teacher putting a hand to the throat can also be a simple method of error correction, communicating to students that they have confused a voiced and unvoiced sound and should try again. The technique is simple enough that it can be quickly integrated into a lesson at any point to remind students of voicing and its impact on meaning.

Aspiration

When the consonant sounds /p/, /t/, and /k/ appear at the start of a word or stressed syllable, we pronounce them with a puff of air; this is called **aspiration**. The word *pie*, for example, could be transcribed as [pʰaɪ]. Without aspiration of the /p/, a listener would hear 'bye'. In general, lack of aspiration in /p/, /t/, and /k/ makes them sound like the voiced /b/, /d/, or /g/, which can seriously affect intelligibility.

Try this ☞ **Demonstrating aspiration**

- Tell your students that you are going to pronounce two words, and they should watch what happens to a piece of paper that you are going to hold in front of your mouth as you say the words.
- Stand sideways to the class, holding the paper loosely just in front of your mouth, and say the word *pie*; the puff of air that is released when /p/ begins a word should make the paper move visibly.
- Now repeat the process but this time say the word *bye*; the students should be able to see that the paper barely moves at all.
- Ask your students to do the same, allowing them to experiment with aspirated sounds. Check whether they have aspirated correctly by observing the movement of the paper.

Why this works ⫸ | Using a visual prop, such as the piece of paper described above, is a quick and effective way of highlighting the puff of air required by aspirated sounds. The visual representation and practice activity is also easy to follow and imitate, and is therefore suitable for all levels of language learner. A final benefit of this technique is that it provides students with a simple way to check their own pronunciation autonomously, using the paper to see aspiration as it happens in real time.

Consonant clusters

A **consonant cluster** is a series of two or more consonant sounds one after the other with no vowel sound to separate them. Consonant clusters can be found at the beginning, middle, or end of a word. There are clusters at the beginning and end of the word *students*, in the middle of the word *description*, and at the end of the word *texts*. Clusters can be challenging for students coming to English from first languages with few or no consonant clusters, such as Japanese. This difficulty causes them to develop coping strategies to make clusters easier to pronounce. The two most usual strategies are:

- omitting one of the consonants in a cluster (e.g. pronouncing *bring* as 'bing' or 'ring')
- inserting a weak, extra vowel sound before or between consonants in the cluster (e.g. making *stop* sound like 'estop' or 'sitop').

Omitting consonants can seriously impact intelligibility and needs attention. Adding weak vowels does not seriously impact intelligibility and is not a priority when the learners' goal is EIL.

Try this ☞ | **Raising awareness of initial consonant clusters and strategies**

In this activity, consonant clusters are introduced by using common adjectives which describe the scene from the window of the classroom.

- Test your students' memory by asking them to tell you, without looking, what can be seen from the window of their classroom. If your classroom has no windows, or very small ones, you could instead briefly show students an image of a view through a window, asking them to tell you what they remember from it.
- Write their answers on the board. They may include words linked to the natural world such as *sky, trees, grass, ground, flowers, plants*; weather vocabulary such as *sunshine, clouds, snow, dry*, or words describing the urban environment including *steps, streets, traffic, crowds*.
- Invite students to go to the classroom window (or look at the picture again) and check if their memory was correct. In a whole-class follow-up, put a tick next to the correctly remembered items and remove the incorrect ones. If they spot any other items not on the list, these should be added.
- Go through each word on the list and underline any consonant clusters that appear at the beginnings of words.

- Point to the first word on your list and say it aloud slowly, asking students how many consonant sounds they hear in the underlined section of each word.
- If students cannot identify the correct number of consonant sounds, say the word and then its cluster again slowly, tracing your finger over each consonant as you pronounce it.
- Go around the class pointing to the words on the board and inviting each student to say them aloud.

✓ *Getting it right*

Initial consonant clusters found at the beginning of words are very important for listeners. If consonants are missed out, it could cause a communication breakdown. If you notice that some students are struggling with the clusters, demonstrate how they can build a word and its cluster bit by bit.
For example, traffic:
ic - ffic - affic - raffic - traffic.

- Extend the activity further by asking students to share with a partner what they wish was outside their classroom window instead of what is there.
- Ask students to share their ideas with the class, adding their new nouns to the list on the board.
- Invite students to read through the new items and tell you if any of them have consonant clusters at the beginning.
- Ask students to pronounce the new vocabulary items with clusters, breaking the words down sound by sound if they struggle to pronounce any.

Try this ☞ **Integrating practice of consonant clusters**

- Assemble a list of words containing consonant clusters. These can be words you have heard your students mispronouncing or examples from a recent reading comprehension or audio/video recording used in class. For example, if in a recent lesson you have watched a video about space, you might take vocabulary from it such as *star*, *space station*, *constellation*, and *planet*.
- Elicit each word as a whole-class retrieval exercise and write them directly up onto the board.
- Ask students to work with a partner saying each word out loud and counting how many consonant sounds they can hear which are right next to each other. Use *star* as an example: star = two consonants at the beginning of the word.
- When everyone has completed the task, invite them to say the word aloud and to tell you how many consonant sounds they have found together and where.
  1. star (two consonants together at the beginning of the word)
  2. space station (two consonants together at the beginning of each word)
  3. constellation (three consonants together in the middle of the word)
  4. planet (two consonants together at the beginning of the word)

 **Getting it right**

As you go through each answer with your students, remind them that clusters at the beginning of words and in the middle are important for intelligibility, and emphasize that they should try not to omit any of the consonants in a cluster. Tell students that if they find the first sound of a cluster particularly difficult (such as the /s/ in *star* or *space station*), they can make the first consonant extra-long to give them time to prepare for the next consonant.

In their attempts to pronounce all of the consonants in a cluster, you might find that some of your students insert a weak *i*- or *e*-like vowel sound before or between two consonants. The word *space*, for example, might sound like 'espace' or 'sipace'. There is no need to correct this; it makes the pronunciation of the cluster easier for your students and the weak inserted vowel seldom threatens intelligibility.

If students are still struggling with the pronunciation of a cluster, go back to the first activity in this chapter, guiding their exploration of what is happening in the mouth when each consonant is pronounced. Once they understand where their tongue should be, or how their lips and mouth should move, it may clarify their understanding and support their articulation.

- Finish the exercise by asking students to work with their partner and think of two more words containing consonant clusters connected to the theme: one must contain a cluster at the beginning of the word and one must have a cluster in the middle.
- Draw a table on the board with two columns. Write 'beginning' into the first and 'middle' into the second.
- Invite students to come up to the board and write their word into the appropriate column, underlining its cluster.
- Ask the students to model their words for the rest of the class, before inviting them to follow their classmate, repeating after them.

Why this works ▶

The technique and the strategies practised in this activity can be drawn upon and integrated into any lesson whenever a vocabulary item with one or more consonant clusters is encountered. Regularly revisiting consonant clusters when they appear in your lesson materials will highlight to students just how common they are in English, justifying the strategies and time spent practising them.

3   Vowels

Teachers and learners often say that vowels are one of the hardest aspects of the pronunciation of English. There seem to be so many vowels in English compared with other languages, and it is much harder to explain how to produce a vowel compared to a consonant. However, when our long-term goal is international intelligibility, there is some good news, and we can help our students by keeping in mind the following points:

- We are not trying to teach them to sound like native speakers. Doing this is not necessary and, in many cases, not desirable, since their accent is a key part of who they are.
- Different native-speaker accents have different 'flavoured' vowels, but they are usually mutually intelligible.
- It is not necessary to be able to produce all 20 vowels of **Received Pronunciation (RP)** in order to be fully intelligible. American, Australian, and New Zealand accents, for example, don't have that many.
- Most learners come to class with enough mother-tongue vowels for them to become internationally intelligible quite quickly.

There are some areas of English vowels that can be problematic:
- Most learners will need to work on vowel length. This includes both the idea of long and short vowels as in *feel* and *fill*, and the shortening effect that voiceless consonants have on the preceding vowel (i.e. the difference between *back* and *bag*).
- The sound–spelling relationships of English vowels are not simple, especially for learners from L1 backgrounds where one written vowel letter corresponds to one vowel sound.
- Coursebooks regularly focus on a standard UK or US accent, but, depending on where you are teaching, it is possible that your own accent, whether native or non-native, is a better model for your students. Speakers with a non-standard accent are tangible proof that you can have 'flavoured' vowels and still be internationally intelligible.

Discriminating between similar vowels

Your students will inevitably find that they struggle with certain vowels. However, the challenge they are experiencing may not be in producing the problem vowel, but in perceiving it. The following two activities can be used to help students distinguish the difference between vowel sounds they hear more clearly.

Try this    **Practising vowel discrimination: Same or different?**

- Before class, prepare two lists of words containing the vowel contrast that you want your students to practise. Some of the pairs of words should be the same, and some pairs should be different by one vowel sound (i.e. minimal pairs), such as *said* and *sad*. The list could look something like this:
  - ♦ said   sad
  - ♦ fed   fed
  - ♦ head   head
  - ♦ bed   bad
  - ♦ bad   bad
  - ♦ said   said
- In class, tell students they are going to hear you say two words. Tell them to listen and to say whether the two words sound the same or different.
- Read the pairs from your list one at a time, stopping to ask 'Same or different?' (If you are working online, you could ask students to do a thumbs up to the camera if they hear the same pronunciation, and thumbs down for a different pronunciation.)
- If students struggle to perceive the target difference, ask them to look at your mouth as you pronounce the words. Depending on the two vowels, they may notice a difference in how open the mouth is, or the shape of the lips (smiling or rounded). Repeat the words if necessary.
- Once the students have given you the answers and you have confirmed or corrected them, say the pairs again, asking students to just listen first of all with the correct answer in mind. Then ask everyone to join you, pronouncing the words together after you.
- Students work with a partner and repeat the task together.
- Ask the pairs to compile their own list, half of which should contain minimal pairs, and half the same word repeated.
- Finally, get one pair of students to join another pair. In turns, each student reads out their list of words while the others listen and decide if the words sound the same or different.

✓ *Getting it right*

This activity is designed to provide students with practice in perceiving the difference between vowels, so it is best if they cannot see the words while listening. Encourage them to trust their ears. You can even ask them to close their eyes if that helps them to focus on the sounds. At the end of your part of the activity, write your words on the board. This is a good moment to draw attention to the typical spellings for each vowel.

Try this    **Categorizing vowel sounds**

Another way in which we can help students to distinguish between vowel sounds is through categorizing. This activity gets students working together to group together words which contain the same vowel.

- Create a list of words you want students to categorize according to their vowel sounds. You could base the list on your observations of their pronunciation in class, or you could take words from a recent reading text, or from an audio script of a listening.

- Put students into groups or pairs. Provide each group with the words on individual cards or slips of paper so that they can physically move them around when categorizing them. If you are working online, using an interactive whiteboard. invite students to drag and drop words to different sections of their screens in accordance with their sound, or to type each word into a designated area. An example of this can be seen in Figure 3.1.

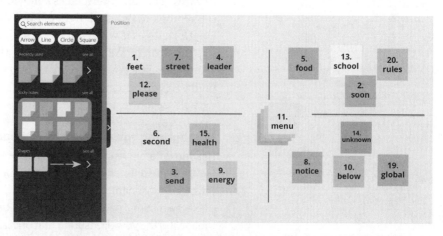

FIGURE 3.1. *Students use Canva's Interactive Whiteboard to categorize words according to the vowel in their stressed syllable*

- Ask them to think about the pronunciation of the vowel sound in each word and group together the words with the same sound. Give a time limit for the activity.
- Before going through the answers, read out each of the words in turn, giving groups the opportunity to listen and make any last-minute changes.
- Run a whole-class feedback session, inviting each student to contribute an answer. If anyone has mis-categorized a word, repeat it, giving them the opportunity to change their answer.

Why this works ▐▐▐▶

In the 'Same or different?' activity, spotting the difference between two words with similar vowels, said only a few seconds apart, is a relatively simple task. However, it is much more difficult to distinguish between similar sounds when you have no audio input to help you, and you have to rely on 'hearing' the sounds in your own head. Because of this, the stage when you pronounce all of the target words is important. Here, learners give their full attention to the words they are not sure of. This type of focused listening is invaluable for long-term learning to happen.

Try this ☞ **Follow-up activity**

Identify a vowel sound that your students find especially problematic. For homework, ask them to bring in cards with words containing that vowel sound. Collect the cards and put them all on a section of the class noticeboard headed 'Vowel of the Month'. When the problem vowel ceases to be a problem, congratulate your students on their improvement and ask them to choose a new one.

Vowel length

English vowels are often classified as being long or short. For example, the vowels in *fish, egg, cat, up, clock, pull* (i.e. /ɪ/, /e/, /æ/, /ʌ/, /ɒ/, and /ʊ/) and the *a* in *ago* (i.e. /ə/) are all described as being short in the RP accent. The other RP vowels are all described as being long, and dictionaries show this with the symbol /ː/. But the length of English vowels is not fixed. One way that length changes is when a vowel is followed by an unvoiced consonant such as /p/, /t/, /s/, or /tʃ/. When this happens, the vowel will be shortened in length. When the same vowel is followed by a voiced consonant, such as /b/, /d/, /z/, or /dʒ/, it will be a little longer. This is true for most English accents and, as we will see in the next activity, is important for intelligibility.

Try this ☞ **Highlighting vowel length by comparing images**

Hearing different lengths of vowels is not easy. This activity uses images to visually highlight the differences in the length of a vowel when followed by a voiced or unvoiced consonant.

- Select a minimal pair that apparently differs only in the consonant sound following the vowel, ensuring that one is voiced and the other unvoiced, as in *back/bag, cap/cab,* or *price/prize*.
- Find one image to represent each word, for example, a picture of a cap and a picture of a (taxi) cab, and show or project both images side by side.
- Invite the students to say what they see in the images, naming the objects out loud.
- Now ask the class what differences they hear between the pronunciations of the two words. They might mention the final consonant sounds, but they probably won't suggest the difference in vowel length. In this case, tell them there is a second difference. Ask them to listen carefully as you pronounce both words again, and to try to identify what it is.
- If students are still struggling to perceive the difference in vowel length, write each noun on the board under its projected image. Make the vowel before the unvoiced consonant appear narrow, and the vowel before the voiced consonant much longer, as shown in Figure 3.2. You could also draw a short or a long arrow under each to highlight their length. Say the nouns again, and ask your students if they notice a difference in the vowel sound now. Finally, explain what is happening and why.

FIGURE 3.2. *Highlighting vowel length visually on the board*

32

Why this works ⫸

It's natural to think that the difference between *cap* and *cab* or *price* and *prize* is a question of the voiceless/voiced nature of the final consonant. However, when voiced consonants come at the end of a word or a stressed syllable, they actually possess little or no voicing. This would seem to suggest that *price* and *prize* should sound the same, but we know they don't. The answer to this enigma lies in vowel length, and studies in phonetics show that the primary difference between *cap/cab* or *price/prize* is the shorter vowel in *cap* and *price*. The same is true for *back* and *bag* or *coat* and *code*, and so on. This shortening effect of the voiceless consonant over the preceding vowel is true for all the voiceless consonants of English in almost all accents, and it is the principal way in which we can distinguish between *cap* and *cab*, *price* and *prize*, and so on. However, this phonetic effect is not common to all languages, and many learners will need considerable help in mastering it in their English.
(This activity was developed from an idea we learned from IATEFL PronSIG colleague, author, and pronunciation expert, Mark Hancock.)

Vowel sounds and spelling

Learners who come to English from a language where one written vowel letter corresponds to one vowel sound in speaking are more likely to have problems with the pronunciation of words they meet on the page. For many young adult and adult learners, the written word is more often than not their first contact with new vocabulary, and is certainly the form in which new vocabulary is kept for learning purposes. Because of this, there is significant value in helping them to decode some of the simple, stable sound–spelling relationships of English vowels.

Try this ☞ **Making sense of the spelling of vowels**

- Before class, go through some recent units in your coursebook and pick out vocabulary that has the alphabet letter that you want to focus on. The letter *o*, for example, often appears in the spelling of the sounds /əʊ/ and /ɒ/.
- Make two lists of the words, one for each vowel sound. For the letter *o*, your lists could look something like this:
- /əʊ/ no, note, go, coat, cold, old, told, close, home, road, toast, wrote
- /ɒ/ on, off, not, got, hot, foggy, clock, want, watch, doctor, shop, coffee
- In class, ask your students to draw a table with two columns. Tell them to put the word 'No' at the head of one column, and the word 'On' at the head of the other column.
- Tell the class that you are going to read out some words that they already know. They have to write each word in either the 'No' or the 'On' column, based on the vowel sound they hear.
- Read out the words, repeating as necessary, and allowing the students time to check with each other after each word. This is not a test: collaboration between students is good, and often leads to requests for you to repeat a word.
- When you have read out all of the words, check the answers. Pronounce a word and invite your students to say 'no' or 'on' accordingly.
- Once the exercise has been marked, select words from one of the columns that follow the same spelling pattern for the vowel sound. For example, from the 'No' column, you could select *note*, *close*, *home*, and *wrote*.

- Ask the students what they notice about the spelling of these 'no' words. Help them to see that all the words contain the sound–spelling pattern '*o*+C+*e*', where C is a single consonant.
- Now invite the students to look for other sound–spelling patterns in the two columns. They should be able to find '*o*+ld' and '*oa*+C' for the 'No' column, and '*o*+C+C', '*a*+C+C' and '*o*+final C' for the 'On' column. If they struggle with this, put the patterns on the board and ask the students to find words with each pattern.

Why this works ▶

> The spelling of English is famous for its irregularities, and to learners it might seem that there are more irregularities than anything else. But this is only true up to a point, and the value of showing your students some of the stronger sound–spelling relationships should not be underestimated. If students know most of the usual spellings of the vowel sounds of English, they do not need to keep looking up the pronunciation in a dictionary. Nor do they need to use the IPA symbols for the sounds of English. IPA is very popular in ELT coursebooks, but it can be a burden for learners who, in the end, have to deal with words and letters on a page. The value of being able to see letters or letter combinations and know how they sound is the driving force behind the **phonics** method, which is used extensively with very young learners. There is no reason, however, to limit a phonics approach to primary and pre-primary learners. It can be just as effective with teenagers and adults.

Understanding how vowels are made

Often, learners are able to pronounce a vowel of English that is not part of their mother-tongue pronunciation just through imitation. Lots of learners can produce /ɑː/ or /ɜː/, in this way. Sometimes, however, neither imitation nor activities to help students perceive vowels are enough. If this happens, students can benefit from articulation exercises that help them to understand:

- the shape of their lips when they produce a specific vowel sound
- how open or closed their mouth needs to be
- where their tongue needs to be in their mouth.

The following task can help learners to understand what they need to do in terms of these three parameters in order to improve their pronunciation of a problem vowel sound.

Try this ☞　**Exploring the vowel space**

- Start the activity by asking your students if they know how they create the different vowel sounds that they pronounce, both in English and in their first language. Accept any answers at this stage. The key to the question is to get your students thinking about how vowel sounds are made.
- Now say the word *he* aloud, and then just its vowel sound, /iː/. Ask the students to join in and do this with you. Repeat this process for *who* and its vowel /uː/.
- Show or project images of lip shapes for /iː/ and /uː/. See Figure 3.3 for an example of this.

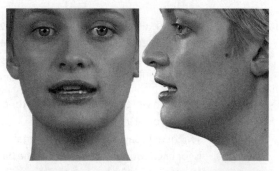

Lip shape in /iː/ as in 'fl**ee**ce'

Lips are spread almost to a smile.

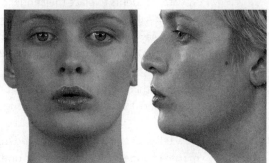

Lip shape in /uː/ as in 'g**oo**se'

Lips are rounded.

FIGURE 3.3.   *Lip shapes for* /iː/ *and* /uː/

- While students are looking at the pictures, get them to make /iː/ and then /uː/ focusing their attention on their lips.
- Ask them which picture shows the lips for the *he* vowel, and which for *who*.
- Get your students to pronounce *he* and *who* again, several times if necessary, focusing on their lips. Now describe these as 'smiling' for /iː/ and 'rounded' for /uː/.
- Next, show or project images of the tongue position for /iː/ and /uː/. See Figure 3.4 for an example of this.

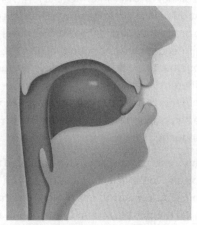

Tongue position for /iː/ in 'fl**ee**ce'

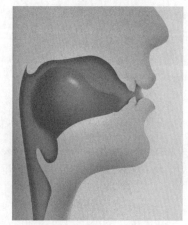

Tongue position for /uː/ in 'g**oo**se'

FIGURE 3.4.   *Tongue positions for* /iː/ *in* '*fleece*' *and* /uː/ *in* '*goose*'

- While your students are looking at the pictures, get them to make /iː/ and then /uː/ sounds as before, but this time focusing their attention on their tongue.
- Ask them what they feel their tongue is doing.

Getting it right   No one is used to thinking about how their tongue moves when they speak, so at first, accept anything that your students tell you about what they feel. Be ready, however, to guide them towards the idea of the tongue being at the front of the mouth for *he* and in the back for *who*.

- Ask them which picture shows the tongue position for the 'he' vowel, and which for the vowel in *who*.
- Tell them to say /iː/ and then /uː/ again, this time focusing on where their tongue is for each sound – at the front or the back of the mouth.
- Now tell students to place their finger on the tip of their tongue and say *can*, and then *car*. Ask them what they notice happening to their tongue. If necessary, get them to say only the vowels, /æ/ and /ɑː/, respectively. They should be able to feel the tongue moving from the front of the mouth towards the back as they go from /æ/ to /ɑː/.
- Point out that the 'can' vowel has the tongue at the front of the mouth (like the 'he' vowel), and the 'car' vowel has the tongue at the back of the mouth, like the 'who' vowel.
- Now tell your students to say *see* and /iː/, and then *sad* and /æ/. Ask them how the mouth changes as they move from one word or vowel to the next. They should notice that their mouth is almost closed for /iː/ and quite open for /æ/. They may notice that their tongue is high up in the mouth for *see*, but moves down for *sad*.
- Finish by inviting your students to tell you the three ways we can move our mouth to make different vowels. They should mention: a) the shape of their lips, b) the position of their tongue, and c) how open their mouth is. Tell them that in future, when they are working on vowels that are a difficult for them, you will refer to these features of the vowel.

Why this works ▶ This activity gets students to think about how we make vowel sounds. At beginner or lower-intermediate levels of English, it will probably be more productive to use imitation or other less cognitive approaches to help students to pronounce different vowels. However, there may come a time when they will need some basic notions of how the tongue, the lips, and the jaw work together to create specific vowels. By using pairs of vowels that have markedly different lip shapes, tongue positions, or jaw positions, and by getting the students to make these sounds while looking at simple pictures, we help them to begin to understand different English vowels without using any technical language.

This same activity can easily be adapted for giving feedback on issues with vowels. Do the activity, focusing only on words that contain the problem sound. Ask your students to focus on what is happening in their mouth, and invite them to play around with tongue and lip positions as they attempt to make the sound.

4 Stress

Stress is a feature of all languages. It is the result of a speaker pronouncing a word, or part of a word, with greater energy and volume than the words or syllables around it. Because of this, the listener perceives the stressed word or syllable as being louder than those around it. The stressed syllable is also longer than it would be if it were not stressed.

In English, stress operates at two levels – at the level of individual words, and at the level of a spoken phrase or sentence. Stress at the level of individual words is commonly known as word stress, although more academic documents will also refer to it as **lexical stress**. In ELT coursebooks and in the classroom, stress at the level of a phrase or complete sentence is commonly referred to as 'sentence stress', while academic descriptions of the phenomenon refer to it as **nuclear stress** or 'tonic stress'.

Word stress

Word stress is a fixed property, and the position of the stressed syllable can be marked in a dictionary. This 'stress mark' usually comes in the form of a small superscript vertical bar before the stressed syllable, as in /ˈleksɪkəl/. While there are some rules students can learn to help them predict where the stress should fall in a word, there are almost as many exceptions. Since incorrect word stress can have a negative impact on intelligibility in English, it is helpful if learners include the correct stress of new words as an integral part of learning vocabulary.

Try this ☞ **Noticing and highlighting stress in words**

- Select a range of words from a recent class which have one, two, or three syllables. For example, for a lower-level class learning food vocabulary, you could choose *bread* and *rice* (both one syllable), *chicken* and *apple* (both two syllables), and *tomato* and *potato* (both three syllables).
- Tell the students you will describe some food items to them and they must guess what they are. Begin by describing the one-syllable items. Once the students have correctly guessed the word *bread*, for example, instruct them to pronounce it with you two more times. Each time you do so, hold up your index finger to represent its single syllable. Repeat the procedure for *rice*.
- Now describe the two-syllable word *chicken*. Once students have correctly guessed, ask them to listen and watch you as you pronounce it. To demonstrate the two-syllables of *chicken*, raise your index finger as you say the first syllable *chick-* and then your middle finger for the second syllable *-en*. Do this twice before asking the students to join you for two more repetitions.

- Now ask the students: Which part of the word is louder and clearer? Repeat the word a few more times. Use your voice to emphasize the stressed syllable and use your fingers to demonstrate the number of syllables.
- Once students have correctly identified the first syllable as being the stressed one, repeat the word two or three more times. You could grab your index finger with your other hand as you pronounce the stressed syllable to further emphasize it. Ask the students to join in for two more repetitions.

✓ Getting it right

Don't overload your students with explanations and terminology when introducing stress. Begin simply with an audible and physical representation of the stressed syllable, allowing them to gradually notice the emphasis occurring in one part of the word only.

- Follow the same procedure for *tomato* and *potato*, raising one finger as you pronounce each syllable, and asking students to listen and identify the stressed syllable, and then pronounce the word as you do.
- Check that students have understood word stress by:
  - ♦ saying words and asking them to use their fingers to show you how many syllables they have, and then pointing to the finger representing the loudest and clearest.
  - ♦ holding up two or three fingers and pointing to the one representing the stressed syllable; students must then volunteer a word which matches this word-stress pattern.
  - ♦ asking them to think of two more foods (or whichever vocabulary items you choose to use) that have the same syllable stress as *bread*, *chicken*, and *tomato*, and to share these with the class.
- As you revisit lexical stress in subsequent lessons, you can start to provide additional visual representations of it alongside written work. For example, when encountering new vocabulary, you can ask students to underline stressed syllables, or to highlight them with a marker pen.

Why this works ⏭

The exact way that word stress operates differs from one language to another, and so some students may struggle to perceive it in English. Actions like holding up a finger, as in the example above, or other physical acts performed at the same time as the emphasized syllable (such as clicking fingers, tapping a pencil, or clapping) can also help students internalize the way in which it is used in English vocabulary.

Try this ☞ **Discovering simple rules for word stress**

Select a short recording with a transcript. Give the students a copy of the transcript with the words to focus on highlighted in bold. Alternatively, ask the students to underline nouns, adjectives, and verbs in the transcript.

✓ Getting it right

It is best to focus on two-syllable words the first time you do this activity, and to choose a recording where a clear majority of nouns and adjectives are stressed on the first syllable, with two-syllable verbs stressed on the second syllable.

- Tell the students to mark the main stress on each of the highlighted words. Then let them listen to the recording, two or three times if necessary, focusing on the words and checking the main stress in each.
- Invite students to check the answers with each other. Then run a whole-class feedback session, with the students saying the target words with the correct stress.
- Ask the students to group words of the same type together (i.e. all of the nouns together, all of the verbs together, etc.). You could give them a grid to write words into, or you could put the words on pieces of paper that students can move around.
- Students work in pairs or groups to write a rule about which syllable is normally stressed in words from each category.
- Invite the students to share their rules. The rules are: two-syllable nouns and adjectives are mostly stressed on the first syllable. Two-syllable verbs are mostly stressed on the second syllable. Discuss exceptions. (Rules about stress in English are never 100% true.) Students add two or three 'obedient' words and one exception to their lists.
- Go around the class listening to the students' additions to their lists.

Why this works ⫸

> Correct word stress can help learners to be better listeners and more intelligible speakers. Word-stress rules in English are very complex. However, with two- and three-syllable nouns, verbs, and adjectives, there are some simple rules that pertain most of the time. Discovering these rules, rather than just being given them, helps learners to internalize them. The discovery process can be applied again at higher levels to determine rules about word stress and prefixes (which are never normally stressed), or word stress and suffixes, where the suffix often determines where the stress will go.

Sentence stress

In English, in a sentence or short phrase, the nouns, verbs, adjectives, and adverbs (i.e. the **content words**) are normally stressed, but the last content word is normally stressed significantly more than the others. In addition, there is a change of pitch (a fall, a rise, a fall-rise. etc.) on this most stressed word in order to highlight it even more.

Correct sentence stress in English is important. For both native-speaker and non-native-speaker listeners, incorrectly placed sentence stress can seriously impact on intelligibility. The most stressed word draws the listener's attention, and so is key to understanding the speaker's message. When the wrong word is stressed, sometimes the listener simply does not understand what the speaker is saying. Worse still, at other times the listener can understand something quite different from what the speaker intended. Either way, communication has failed.

Try this    **Which kinds of words are stressed?**

- Ask your students to listen to you as you chant the following sentences, clapping on the words in bold as you do so.

Kids sing songs.

The kids sing songs.

The kids are singing songs.

The kids are singing the songs.

The kids have been singing the songs.

- Now ask the students to listen again, paying attention to the words you clap on; what type of words are they? The students may be able to identify that you clap on content words (nouns and verbs in this example, but this could also include adjectives and adverbs), which contain important information for the listener.
- Ask the students to listen again, but to pay attention to the words that you do not clap on: are they also content words? The students may be able to tell you that the non-clapped words are articles and modal verbs. These types of words are 'function words' or 'grammar words', and they connect the content words.
- Ask the students to join in with you chanting the lines and clapping.
- Now put the words on the board or screen and ask the students to repeat the chant (while clapping) two more times. This time they can read the words if they wish.
- Once the chanting has finished, elicit from students (or point out):
  - ♦ How many times they clapped for each line (three times).
  - ♦ The length of each line: was it the same or different? It should be visible to the students that although the number of function words increased in each line, they still only clapped on the same three content words.
  - ♦ The sound of the clapped versus the non-clapped words; were they clear and easy to hear? The students might have observed that they were forced to pronounce the function words much more rapidly in order to fit around the three clapped content words, making them less clear.

✔ *Getting it right*

At first, don't show the students the written chant. Let them listen several times, perceiving the difference between stressed and unstressed words by ear. The emphasis and clapping on the content words should be enough for them to differentiate between content and function words before they have even looked at the chant on the page.

Why this works ▶

This activity allows students first to perceive the way stress is used in different types of words, and then to discover a simple rule. Typically, we stress content words, making them clearer and easier to hear, and we don't stress function words such as prepositions, articles, or auxiliary verbs. In fact, some speakers, particularly native speakers, weaken their pronunciation significantly, which makes them harder to hear. However, learners using English for international communication shouldn't try to pronounce function words like native speakers do. Doing so can make them less intelligible. That said, being aware of how these altered function words sound will help learners understand what native speakers are saying.

Try this 👉 **The most stressed word**

Once students are aware of which kinds of words are normally stressed in spoken English, we can go on and introduce the idea of a 'most stressed' word. This 'most stressed' word, which is called the tonic, plays an important role in successful communication. The easiest way to introduce it is through simple, short sentences.

- Show your students a selection of familiar phrases or short sentences. For beginners or elementary students, these could be simple statements and questions such as: *I'm from Thailand, This is my brother, I like playing tennis, I live in Manchester, What's your name?, How old are you?, What time is it?, Do you like classical music?, I need some new shoes.*

✓ *Getting it right*

It is best to use phrases or short sentences that your learners are familiar with, preferably from recent classwork. Being familiar with the selected phrases allows learners to give full attention to the pronunciation focus of the activity. Unfamiliar vocabulary or structures will distract them.

- Remind students about sentence stress. Check to see if they remember that English normally stresses content words (nouns, adjectives, verbs, and adverbs). Invite students to say each of the selected phrases aloud with good sentence stress. Correct where necessary.
- Now ask the class how many words were stressed in each statement or question. Point out that sometimes only one word is stressed (e.g. *I'm from Thailand.*), but that often two or even three words are stressed (e.g. *This is my brother. / How old are you? / I need some new shoes.*).
- Explain that when there are two or more stressed words in a sentence, one of them is stressed more than the others, and that is the most important word in the speaker's message.
- Now ask the students to listen to you while you model one of the phrases with two or three stressed words. Ask them to identify the most stressed word in each sentence. Repeat the modelling if necessary. Check their answers, and then repeat the modelling with the other sentences.
- When you have modelled all of the sentences, invite the class to suggest a simple rule to explain which word is the most stressed in sentences and questions like these. Congratulate your students if they then come up with the right rule. If they don't, give them the rule. (In English, the most stressed word in a phrase or short sentence is normally the last content word.)
- Show the students a new set of five or six phrases or short sentences that they are already familiar with. Ask them to identify the last content word. Check their answers and then invite them to say each example with good sentence stress. Correct if necessary.

Try this 👉 **Sentence stress in dialogues**

Coursebooks are full of dialogues. After you have used a dialogue in the way set out in the coursebook, you can go back to it a week or so later and use it again to practise sentence stress. In particular, reinforce the idea of stress falling on content words, and the way in which the main stress normally, but not always, falls on the last content word.

- Ask students two or three simple questions about a dialogue that they worked on recently so as to remind them of who was talking to whom, and what happened. Direct them to the script of the dialogue in the coursebook. Play the recording of the dialogue while the students listen and read.

- Ask students what they can remember about which words are normally stressed in spoken English, and use their answers to re-affirm that it is normally the content words (i.e. nouns, verbs, adjectives, and adverbs). Remind the class about the 'most stressed word' in a spoken phrase, and elicit from them that it is normally the last content word.
- Students work in pairs. They go through the transcript of the dialogue underlining stressed words and double-underlining the most stressed word.

Sample dialogue

Shop assistant:	Can I help you?
Rob:	Yes, what size is this shirt?
Shop assistant:	Let's see. It's a small. What size do you need?
Rob:	A medium.
Shop assistant:	This is a medium.
Rob:	Thanks. Where can I try it on?
Shop assistant:	The changing rooms are over there.
Rob:	Thank you.

(FROM ENGLISH FILE 4ᵀᴴ ED. ELEMENTARY. PRACTICAL ENGLISH, EPISODE 3)

- When students are ready, play the recording again. Give them a minute or so to make any changes, and then show them the dialogue with the correct sentence stress marked on it.

Sample dialogue

Shop assistant:	Can I <u>help</u> you?
Rob:	Yes, <u>what</u> <u>size</u> is this <u><u>shirt</u></u>?
Shop assistant:	<u>Let's</u> <u>see</u>. It's a <u>small</u>. <u>What</u> <u>size</u> do you <u>need</u>?
Rob:	A <u>medium</u>.
Shop assistant:	<u>This</u> is a medium.
Rob:	<u>Thanks</u>. <u>Where</u> can I <u>try</u> it <u>on</u>?
Shop assistant:	The <u>changing</u> <u>rooms</u> are <u>over</u> <u>there</u>.
Rob:	<u>Thank</u> you.

(FROM ENGLISH FILE ELEMENTARY. PRACTICAL ENGLISH, EPISODE 3).

- Deal with any differences your students have between their answers and the answers you have shown them. They may ask why the main stress is on 'This' in 'This is a medium'. Explain that stressing 'This' draws Rob's attention to the shirt that the shop assistant has just found.

 **Getting it right**

Although the most stressed word is normally the last content word, there are occasions when this is not the case. For example, when the shop assistant says 'This is a medium', they will be holding out a shirt to give to Rob. 'This' is the most important word in this situation because it directs the listener's attention to the shirt the shop assistant is holding up. There is no need to go into any theory here. The important message is that the most stressed word is normally the last content word, but there are exceptions.

- Invite the students to practise the dialogue focusing on producing correct sentence stress. Finally, if you wish, tell the students to record the dialogue with a partner as part of their mark for pronunciation for that part of their course (see Chapters 7 and 10).

Why this works ▮▮▮➡

Sentence stress in English is complex, especially once we move from isolated sentences to full dialogues. However, the importance of sentence stress in achieving intelligibility means that it cannot be left to sort itself out. It is essential that learners become aware of the way sentence stress works, particularly the idea of the most stressed word normally being the last content word. From this basic rule, they will be in a position to do two things:

a) get the main stress right most of the time in their own speech, and so improve their intelligibility.

b) notice when the stress in somebody else's speech falls on a word other than the last content word, and to wonder why this has happened. This prepares them for the next stage: using sentence stress deliberately to create specific meanings for specific situations.

Part 3　Teaching techniques

5   The learner's L1

Until recently, the default goal for teaching English pronunciation has been to get as close as possible to a native-speaker accent. The learner's mother tongue has inevitably been seen as an obstacle in this process, or as a source of bad habits that need to bc ovcrcomc. However, with international intelligibility as a goal (see Chapter 1), the learner's first-language pronunciation can be seen in a different light. Rather than insisting that our students 'leave their mother tongue at the door' when they come to class, we can (and should) ask them to bring it into the room with them, and to get ready to use it in order to improve their pronunciation of English. In short, we and our students need to see the mother tongue as friend, and not foe, as a resource and not as an obstacle.

The benefits of deliberately bringing our students' L1 into the classroom are two-fold. Firstly, it allows us to identify the features of English pronunciation that are priorities for international intelligibility but that are not part of our students' first-language phonology. Secondly, it allows us to access sounds and other features that *are* part of the L1, and that our learners can already pronounce. Because they are part of their L1 pronunciation, these features can be brought out into the open and used to pronounce target features of English.

The benefits to be gained from using the learners' L1 apply mostly to classes where the students share the same mother tongue, and where the teacher speaks this language and knows about its pronunciation and its different accents. But even in classes where students speak different first languages, it is possible to adapt activities to the needs of the group.

Getting your priorities right

There are plenty of lists online and in teachers' manuals detailing the pronunciation problems that learners of English are likely to encounter depending on their first language. If your learners' mother tongue is Korean, for example, you will find lists of the pronunciation problems for Korean-L1 speakers who are learning English. Almost without exception, these lists are based on what is problematic for learners who are aiming for a native-speaker accent. However, when our goal is international intelligibility, it is the Lingua Franca Core (LFC; the list of pronunciation features that research has indicated are central to being intelligible in international communication in English; see Appendix 1) that guides our teaching priorities. By comparing the LFC with traditional lists of problems for your learners, you can get a precise idea as to where your learners' pronunciation priorities lie.

Try this ☞ **English as an International Language (EIL) pronunciation priorities for my students**

- Draw a table with four columns, as shown in Table 5.1.

Areas of pronunciation	Features of international intelligibility (EIL)	Traditional (EFL) problems for [French, Chinese, Spanish, etc.] speakers	EIL priorities for [French, Chinese, Spanish, etc.] speakers
Consonants			
Clusters			
Vowels			
Word stress			
Sentence stress			
Rhythm			
Intonation			

TABLE 5.1.   *Determining priorities for international intelligibility*

- Complete Column 2 (Features of international intelligibility) with the LFC pronunciation features, i.e. the ones that are important for international intelligibility. If you cannot remember them, do your best, and then check your ideas against the priorities shown in Appendix 1.
- Complete Column 3 (Traditional (EFL) problems) with the problems that speakers with your students' first language are traditionally said to have with English pronunciation.

 **Getting it right** As mentioned above, you can find lists of pronunciation problems for different L1 backgrounds online or in teachers' handbooks, but your own classroom experience is just as valuable, so don't hesitate to add these to Column 3.

- Finally, compare the two columns that you have filled in. Anything that features in both columns is a priority for international intelligibility and should be written into Column 4 (EIL priorities). Make any additional notes that help you to understand the reasoning behind each priority for your students.

 **Getting it right** This is an activity that is best done by you as a teacher, rather than by your students in class. Better still, try doing it together with your colleagues in the English department. The activity will reveal the areas of English pronunciation that need the most attention if your students are aiming for international intelligibility.

Why this works ⫸ This activity prompts us to think carefully about what the priorities are for our own students, taking into account their L1 pronunciation. As an example, Table 5.2 has been completed for a selection of consonants and vowels that are usually problematic for French speakers of English. However, Column 3 can be adapted to any first language, which will then produce different priorities in Column 4.

Areas of pronunciation	Features of international intelligibility (EIL)	Traditional (EFL) problems for [French, Chinese, Spanish, etc.] speakers	EIL priorities for [French, Chinese, Spanish, etc.] speakers
Consonants	Consonants are a priority area, with the exceptions of /θ/, /ð/, and /r/, where a number of variations are acceptable.	French speakers don't generally aspirate /p/, /t/, and /k/ at the beginning of words.	**Priority.** Aspiration of word-initial /p/, /t/, and /k/ is important in EIL.
		/tʃ/ and /dʒ/ do not exist in French and are often pronounced as /ʃ/ and /ʒ/.	**Priority.** The correct pronunciation of most consonants is important in EIL.
		The 'th' sounds /θ/ and /ð/, as in *think* and *then*, are often pronounced as /s/ and /z/ by European French speakers, or as /t/ and /d/ by French Canadians.	**Not a priority.** The sounds /s/ and /t/ are internationally intelligible variations of /θ/, as are /z/ and /d/ for /ð/.
		Some French speakers pronounce English /r/ in their throat. Others use a trilled sound.	**Not a priority.** Both variations of /r/ are intelligible, though the trill is generally more easily understood.
Vowels	Differences in vowel length are important. Variation in vowel quality is not so problematic, provided that the quality of a speaker's vowels is consistent. (For more detail of vowel length and quality, see Chapter 3).	French speakers often pronounce *fill* in such a way that it sounds like *feel*.	**Partial priority.** The sounds /ɪ/ and /iː/ are different in both length and quality, but most practice work should concentrate on the difference in length.
		French speakers often make *paper* sound like *pepper*.	**Partial priority.** The sounds /eɪ/ and /e/ are different in length and quality. Practice should focus on producing a long /e/ for *paper* and a very short /e/ for *pepper*.
		French speakers do not shorten vowels before voiceless consonants.	**Priority.** Vowel length differences are important in EIL.
		French speakers tend to produce full vowels in unstressed syllables instead of a weak schwa sound /ə/.	**Not a priority.** The use of schwa in unstressed syllables is not recommended for EIL, since it can make the speaker less intelligible than if they were using the full vowel. See Appendix 1 for more details.

TABLE 5.2.   *Priorities for international intelligibility: completed for a selection of consonants and vowels that are usually problematic for French speakers of English*

The results of 'filtering' traditional lists of problems for a given L1 through the features of international intelligibility can be quite surprising. Most teachers of French-L1 students, for example, will initially be reluctant to ignore their students' pronunciation of the *th* sounds, or to disregard their lack of schwas in unstressed syllables. But the filtering activity clearly shows that these two key features of native-speaker pronunciation are not priority areas for the goal of international intelligibility.

The L1 as the starting point

The simplest way to make use of the learners' mother tongue is to identify a sound or some other feature of pronunciation that the students already produce in their first language, and then to use this as the starting point for work on a problematic target sound or feature of English.

Mandarin Chinese, for example, has /f/ but not /v/, which can be a real problem for Chinese students learning English. Similarly, Spanish-L1 students come to class with /s/ but not /z/. In both cases, we are looking at a problem of voicing: /v/ and /z/ are the voiced 'partners' of /f/ and /s/, respectively. However, since our learners can already pronounce /f/ or /s/, all we need to do is help them to add voicing to their L1 sound. (See Chapter 2 for more on voicing.)

Try this    **Adding voicing**

This activity helps your students to add voicing to a voiceless consonant from their L1 in order to pronounce a voiced consonant of English. The example uses /f/ to make /v/, and will work for students from any first language that has /f/ but not /v/, and for any language that has a voiceless sound but not its voiced equivalent.

- Ask students to place their thumb and first finger on their throat, as in Figure 5.1.

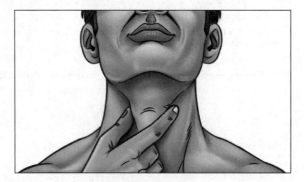

FIGURE 5.1.   *Placing the thumb and first finger on the throat to test for voicing*

- Now ask them to imitate you. Make the buzzing sound of a bee (a continuous /z/). Ask your students what they can feel in their throat with their hand when they make the same sound.

✓ Getting it right   Your students might need to use their first language to be able to say what they feel. Don't worry about this; encourage them to say anything they want. There are no wrong answers at this stage.

- Next, ask students to make a long /s/ with their hand over their throat. As they are making the long /s/, ask them if they notice any difference in their throat compared to the /z/. As before, encourage all answers at this stage.
- Next, get your class to make a long /s/, but to switch to /z/ after a few seconds, and then back to /s/ and then back to /z/, and so on for as long as their breath lasts. Once again, ask your students what the difference is in their throat between the two sounds.
- Explain to the class that in all languages, some sounds are voiced (i.e. there is

vibration in the throat while the sound is being made). The sound /z/ is voiced. In contrast, some sounds are not voiced (i.e. there is no vibration). Introduce the term 'voiceless' for sounds like /s/ that are made without any vibration. (If your students are already familiar with voiced and voiceless sounds and have done the 'Try this' exercise on page 23, you can skip the previous steps).

- Next demonstrate /f/ and /v/ for your students. Produce a long /f/ sound, and then switch into a /v/, putting your hand over your throat for the /v/. Repeat to see if your students have spotted the difference in voicing. Finally, make a very long sound where you alternate the two:
/fffvvvfffvvvfffvvvfffvvv/, putting your hand over your throat for /v/ and taking it off for /f/.
- Ask students to imitate you with a very long alternating sound:
/fffvvvfffvvvfffvvvfffvvv/. Make sure that they have their hand over their throat to test for voicing in /v/ and the lack of voicing in /f/.
- Finally, invite them to make a long /v/ without starting from /f/. When they have done this, congratulate them. Point out that because /f/ is a sound in their mother tongue, they can use it to help them make /v/, which is a problematic sound for them in English.

Why this works ▌▌▌➡

> Once your students understand voicing (see Chapter 2) and are able to add voicing at will, they can use mother-tongue sounds like /p/, /t/, /k/, /f/, /s/, or /tʃ/ to successfully pronounce voiced consonants like /b/, /d/, /g/, /v/, and so on. The reverse process is also possible, i.e. learners can start from a voiced L1 consonant and remove voicing to produce a voiceless English consonant.

Searching for hidden sounds

All languages contain 'hidden' sounds. These are sounds that are not phonemes of the language, but which occur naturally in certain contexts. The sound /ŋ/, for example, is quite common in English (as found in *sing*, *finger*, *going*, etc.) but is not a phoneme in many other languages. However, it does appear in many languages as a natural variation of /n/. This is the case of the *n* in the Spanish word *banco* or the French word *dingue*.

Try this ☞ **I didn't realize I did that!**

The key to this technique is to start from the students' first language and to use it to 'discover' the target sound hidden there. In the case of /ŋ/, for example, you need to find a word where a letter *n* is followed by /k/ or /g/. This happens in Polish in the word *tankowac* (meaning to fill up a car). We will use *tankowac* here as an example of how to do the activity. (The activity will work for other first languages, of course. For Spanish-L1 students you could use *banco*, for French-L1 you could use *dingue*, for Japanese, *sangai*, and so on.)

- Ask students to pronounce *tankowac*, first normally, and then gradually lengthening the *n* so that they eventually produce '*tannnnnnnnkowac*'.
- Now tell the students to do the same again, but to stop just before actually pronouncing the *k*. Model for them by pronouncing *tannnnnn(k)* where *(k)* represents the /k/ sound that you form in the mouth but do not pronounce.
- Now model *tannnnn(k)* followed by the English past simple word *sang* /sæŋ/. Do this two or three times and then ask your students to imitate you.

 **Getting it right**　　Most students aren't used to focusing their attention on what is happening inside their mouths, so it might be useful at this stage to show them a picture of the articulation of /ŋ/. This will help them to realize that for the *n* in *tankowac*, the back of the tongue is raised to the area at the back of the roof of the mouth.

- Tell them that English words like *sang* end in the same way as the *n* they were pronouncing in Polish in *tankowac*. Ask them for other English words that end like *sang*. Expect words like *bang, bring, sing, song, going, doing*, etc.
- Stress how Polish has helped them with a common sound of English. Show them the IPA symbol for the new sound if your students are familiar with IPA. If they aren't, give the new sound a name such as 'the back of the mouth *n*'.
- Practise saying English words with final /ŋ/ before going on to practise listening to and pronouncing minimal pairs like *sin/sing* or *ban/bang*, etc.

Why this works ▓▓▶

In English, the sounds /n/ and /ŋ/ are different phonemes and create different words, as in the case of *ban* and *bang*. In contrast, in many other languages, /n/ and /ŋ/ are just variations of the same sound (i.e. allophones). In these languages, when /n/ is followed by /k/ or /g/, it is pronounced /ŋ/ rather than /n/. That is to say, the English phoneme /ŋ/ is actually formed repeatedly in the mouths of learners of English from different L1 backgrounds without their being aware of it. This activity makes them aware of what they are doing, and then actively transfers the /ŋ/ from the learner's L1 environment to its environment in English. This transfer technique avoids the need for verbal explanations of the articulation of /ŋ/ and highlights the value of the L1 when working on the pronunciation of English.

Try this ☞　**I have a friend who does that**

Not all of the sounds of English can be found hidden away in the learner's L1 like the /ŋ/. However, regional accents of the learner's L1 may use the English sound that is missing from the students' English. For example, the sound /dʒ/ is not a phoneme of Portuguese, but the São Paulo accent of Brazilian Portuguese uses /dʒ/ for the *d* of *bom día*. The same happens with /ʃ/ in Spanish. Although /ʃ/ is not a phoneme of Spanish, it is found in regional languages like Catalan, Galician, or Asturian, and so can be accessed via them for use in English. To access /ʃ/, for example, with learners whose L1 is Spanish:

- Show the class a selection of words from one of the regional languages that uses /ʃ/. With Galician, this could be *xente* (people), *caixa* (savings bank), or *baixo* (low). Ask students to pronounce these words, and then ask them to isolate the pronunciation of the letter *x*, and to try to pronounce this on its own.
- Tell the students that the sound made when pronouncing the *x* in Galician language words is very similar to the sound made when trying to pronounce *sh* in English words. Contrast *xente* with *shed*, *caixa* with *cash*, and so on, getting your students to imitate you and to focus their attention on the transfer of the Galician *x* to the English *sh*.
- Working entirely in English, practise the pronunciation of words containing /ʃ/ in initial, medial, and final position in a word (e.g. *ship, fishing, wish*).
- At a later date, work with minimal pair exercises that contrast /s/ and /ʃ/, (e.g. *sign/ shine*), and then go on to contrast /s/, /ʃ/, and /tʃ/, as in *sip, ship*, and *chip*.

Why this works ▐▐▐➡ | As with all of the activities in this chapter, the key to success is the fact that the target English sound is available to the students through, in this case, a regional language or dialect that is closely related to their first language. The activity places great value on what the students can already do, and simply encourages them to do the same thing when speaking English. Obviously, the more you know about your learners' L1 phonology, the easier it is for you to carry out the previous activities.

Try this  **Playing with bilingual accents**

Most students are fairly good at imitating the way that native speakers of English pronounce their first language. It is generally a source of great amusement to imitate these speakers, but it can also be a route to target sounds of English. By getting our students to imitate an English-L1 speaker of their own language, we can get them to inadvertently use the English articulation for target sounds. For example, the Spanish word *tetera* (teapot) said with an English accent causes Spanish-L1 speakers to use the alveolar /t/ of English in place of the dental /t/ of Spanish. Similarly, when *dedo* (finger) is said with an English accent, this causes Spanish speakers to use an English, alveolar /d/ rather than their natural dental /d/.

In class with your students:

- Choose one or two words that contain the sound you want to practise. Here, as an example, we will use *tetera* from Spanish, but you will need to use a word or words from your students' own L1.
- Pronounce the L1 words with an English accent. Your English pronunciation of these L1 words will invariably produce laughter. Now ask your students if they can do the same, that is, speak their mother tongue with an English accent.
- When they have shown you that they can do this (they do it uncomfortably well for many native-speaker teachers of English!), get them to focus on what is happening with their lips or with their tongue inside their mouth in order for them to pronounce the sample words with the two different accents. In the case of *tetera*, for example, the position of the tip of their tongue when they speak English-accented Spanish (i.e. tongue tip on the alveolar ridge) is quite different from their normal Spanish tongue position, which is the front of the tongue against the back of the top teeth.

✓ *Getting it right* | With consonants, it can help to show your students face diagrams of the L1 and English-accented target sounds. Most students quickly see which diagram represents which accent. With vowels, students often come up with quite odd descriptions of how they make the L1 version of a word as opposed to the English-accented version. The 'oddness' is not important. What matters is that they can describe the difference.

- Next, say a sentence or phrase in English with the target sound(s). With /t/, for example, you could say 'tea for two'. Do this first with an English accent, and then with an accent reflecting your students' L1. With Spanish-L1 students, for example, this would mean pronouncing the words *tea* and *two* first with English alveolar /t/ and then with Spanish dental /t/.
- As before, the L1–accented version of an English word will generate a definite reaction from your students, but perhaps a more uncomfortable laugh than when they heard the English-accented version of their own mother-tongue words.

- Now get the class to work in pairs playing deliberately with both L1-accented and English-accented versions of the target sound in a simple sentence. The listener has to say which accent they think is being used.
- End the activity by pointing out to your students that in the previous step they demonstrated that they are perfectly capable of pronouncing the target English sound(s) with both an L1-influenced and an English accent. Congratulate them for having bilingual accents, but tell them that in the future, you only want them to use the English version when speaking English.

Why this works ▊▊▊➡

By drawing on their ability to imitate an L1 English person pronouncing their mother tongue, your students are able to access the correct pronunciation of a target English sound. It then only remains for them to make the target sound when speaking English. The transition to the point at which the students automatically make the target sound correctly is often slow, and requires constant practice. However, the students now have an easy starting point, thanks to this bilingual accent activity.

6 Pronunciation and technology

Pronunciation teaching has used technology for a long time now; today's technology, however, is more sophisticated and, potentially, more useful to learners. Some of today's technologies have been specifically developed for teaching pronunciation, and are part of what is known as computer-assisted pronunciation teaching (**CAPT**). However, although CAPT is now increasingly available to help individual learners to work autonomously on improving their pronunciation, it does have its drawbacks. For example, CAPT apps almost always focus on the goal of a native-speaker accent, rather than on the more achievable, and globally more useful, goal of international intelligibility. In addition, good quality CAPT apps cost money, usually paid on a monthly or yearly basis via a credit card.

An alternative to CAPT are apps that are not specifically designed for practising pronunciation, but that are accessible through smartphones, making them a realistic option for learners all over the world. For example, most of today's phones have an app built into the operating system that uses automatic speech recognition (ASR). The user speaks into the phone and their words are converted into text. As ASR technology improves, the text it produces increasingly reflects the user's intelligibility as opposed to their nearness to a native-speaker accent. Another, more universally accessible, resource is the internet. Through it, students can hear English spoken by hundreds of competent speakers in multiple different accents. The teaching potential of these two relatively simple technologies is enormous.

Accessing different accents

Students in shared-L1 classes (i.e. classes where all the students speak the same first language) don't get enough exposure to English spoken in a variety of accents. They can often understand English spoken with their own accent, when in fact that accent would not be intelligible to listeners coming from a different L1 background. To overcome this problem, teachers working in shared-L1 environments need to give their students access to speakers with different accents from their own.

Try this ☞ **A window on the world**

The internet is an example of everyday technology that allows us to access a wealth of authentic spoken material in countless different accents, both native and non-native.

- Find a suitable source of recordings of English speakers from different L1 backgrounds. The source could be online platforms such as ELLLO (the English Listening Lesson Library Online), IDEA (the International Dialects of English Archive; see Appendix 4 for details), or the OUP teacher's handbook *Teaching the Pronunciation of English as a Lingua Franca*.
- Select two or three short recordings, preferably about the same topic.

✓ Getting it right

Use short recordings. Two minutes is enough; more will lead to overload and your students could disengage. Try to find recordings where the speakers have markedly different accents, such as French, Japanese, and Arabic.

- Prepare your students for listening in the usual way, getting them to talk about their own experience of, or opinions about, the topic covered in the recordings. Pre-teach any key vocabulary if necessary.
- Let them listen to each recording in turn, checking their general comprehension but not worrying too much about small details. Encourage the students to react at a personal level to what they have just heard by sharing their opinions on the topic, or by telling their partners about any similarities or differences they have noted when comparing the content with their own experiences.
- Invite further comments about which speaker they found to be the easiest or most difficult to understand.
- Finish by asking the class how they think other speakers of English perceive their accent – easy/difficult to understand; nice to listen to, etc.

Why this works ▐▐▐▶

If you choose a topic that interests your students, they will engage with the content rather than worry about the accents. Choose recordings of speakers that your students will find broadly intelligible. The activity will open a window into the world of English as an international language. At the same time, it will demonstrate that while speakers have quite different accents, intelligibility is not seriously at risk. It might also prompt your students to reflect on how they are perceived by their listeners when they use English for international communication. Of course, your students may find that some speakers are easier to understand than others. This is normal. It is important, however, that they get used to listening to speakers with different accents, and a large part of Chapter 7 goes into how we can help our students do this.

Try this ☞ **Real-time communication**

Establish your own online international English language exchange, where students can meet and practise English with learners from around the world.

- Locate a teacher in another country with students who are similar to yours in age, language level, and goals to help facilitate the exchange. Consider teaching friends, acquaintances, colleagues, or partner organizations linked to the school where you teach.
- Select a convenient online platform that will enable everyone to meet. Ensure that it provides breakout rooms for group work and pair work.
- In advance of the meeting, liaise with your exchange counterpart to produce a range of appropriate conversational topics and questions that the students will discuss. These could be linked to recent lesson themes or they could simply be common conversational topics which students will have thoughts and opinions on, for example movies, music, hobbies, family, or jobs.

✓ Getting it right

If students are reticent and you notice a lot of silences, consider providing tasks which are a little more structured, challenging, and collaborative. The following activities can be prepared with students' L1 or particular pronunciation difficulties in mind, providing practice in selected sound features. Consider:

- a spot-the-difference task, where all the objects in the picture contain the specific sound features you wish the students to practise; students must work collaboratively to identify these.
- a map task, where students direct each other through streets and around buildings, all of which could contain pre-selected sound features intended for practice.
- a student–student dictation paragraph containing pre-selected sounds: students read the sentences aloud to their partner, who writes down exactly what they hear. Such a task highlights any sounds that are not produced intelligibly, and which subsequently require clarification and extra practice.

Why this works ⟫

Online international English exchanges can offer many benefits to learners: they allow them to put their new linguistic knowledge into practice in a natural communicative setting, something which many students complain they don't have enough opportunity to do. They also highlight the important skill of **accommodation**, where, cued by a puzzled expression or request for repetition, students often have to modify their pronunciation to better support their partner's comprehension. Finally, they demonstrate how varied international accents of English can be, allowing students to become accustomed to their diversity.

Giving marks and feedback

Learner surveys have shown that students place a great deal of importance on pronunciation. Sometimes they wonder why it doesn't receive a mark in the same way as other areas of English. The easiest way to remedy this situation is to get your students to record their pronunciation work and then to send it to you for marking and comments. Making a recording is a non-threatening way of working on pronunciation, and any feedback is individualized.

Note that as we saw in the introduction to this chapter, for immediate, individualized feedback, students can experiment with the ASR app built into their smartphones.

Try this ☞ Recording pronunciation for marking

- Tell the class that you want them to make a recording of a pronunciation exercise, or of a monologue or dialogue they have just worked on in their coursebook. Check that everyone can access a smartphone, laptop, or desktop computer that can make and send digital voice recordings.

**Getting it right**

When you do this activity for the first time, choose a pronunciation exercise that gives the students a clear and specific pronunciation focus. Once they are used to making recordings, you can get them to record monologues or dialogues. This integrates pronunciation into other areas of learning English.

- Put the students to work in pairs or small groups in class, practising the chosen exercise, monologue, or dialogue, and identifying any significant pronunciation problems they have.
- While students are working in pairs or groups, encourage them to critique each other's pronunciation. At the same time, go around offering help as needed. Finally, have students practise the most significant pronunciation problems you have identified as a whole class.
- Now explain the marking system you are going to use for the recordings. It is important that students understand what the focus of the exercise is, and realize that they won't lose marks for mistakes that are unrelated to this focus.
- Ask the students to each make a recording of the exercise, monologue, or dialogue in their own time at home or in school. Give them a deadline for sending the recordings to your email address. Remind them to say their name at the beginning of the recording.
- With a separate copy of the script for each student, indicate 'Very good', 'Good', 'Not so good', and 'Wrong' using symbols such as ✓✓, ✓, ?, and ✗, so that each student has an individualized record of where their pronunciation is good and where it needs improvement.

Why this works ⫸

Recording students' pronunciation and giving an overall mark for each exercise they record allows you to build up a course mark over an extended period of time for each individual student. Giving the students some initial time in class to work on the recording allows you to uncover general problems and deal with them in class. It also allows students to feed back to their peers. This is valuable because it helps them to be both critical and supportive of each other at the same time. Finally, focusing on only one or two pronunciation points reduces the stress students can feel when making the recording.

Try this ☞ **Feedback from automatic speech recognition (ASR)**

As we suggested in the introduction to this chapter, the ASR on a smartphone can be used for teaching pronunciation. One good reason for doing this is that it gives students individual feedback. Another is the fact that students work with their phones in private, rather than having to attempt to pronounce English in front of the rest of the class.

- Using a short text from work that you have been doing recently in class, students work individually using the ASR/dictation facility on their smartphone to produce a written message from what they say.
- If the transcript the phone produces is an exact (or very good) replica of the text the students dictated to the phone, congratulate them and invite them to repeat the dictation activity using a different text.

**Getting it right**

Once they have done the first text successfully, allow students to choose other short texts taken from recent classwork. Encourage them to look for texts containing words and phrases that they find hard to pronounce. Choosing their own texts will motivate students more than if the teacher chooses one for them.

- If their first attempt results in quite a lot of mistakes, point out that this is because their pronunciation needs improving. Ask the students for examples of the 'mistakes' the phone text has. The 'Student's dictated text' below gives an idea of the sort of mistakes ASR makes when a speaker's pronunciation needs work.
- Put the most common mistakes on the class board, and discuss what the pronunciation problems might be. Give the students help with the correct pronunciation of the most significant mistakes, and then invite them to repeat the exercise, taking care with these pronunciations in particular. While the students are making their second attempt, go round the class helping individual students where necessary.

Original text

How to make garlic soup

Take two cloves of garlic, peel them, and chop them up quite fine. Fry the garlic in a little bit of olive oil. You can add chilli pepper if you want the soup to be spicy.

Student's dictated text

('Mistakes' in the app's output are shown in greyed-out text.)

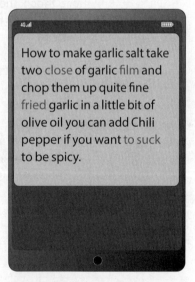

How to make garlic salt take two close of garlic film and chop them up quite fine fried garlic in a little bit of olive oil you can add Chili pepper if you want to suck to be spicy.

Seeing is believing

One problem with learning and practising pronunciation is that learners are not always able to identify their own errors. With word and sentence stress, for example, there can be a gap between what a student thinks they are stressing and where they are actually putting the stress. Students can perceive themselves as saying LONdon or What TIME is it? when in fact they are actually saying lonDON and What time is IT? Students with this perception problem can benefit from visual feedback, and this can be provided by a smartphone voice-recording app that produces a waveform of the words being recorded. A number of smartphone apps do this.

Try this    **Taking a look at stress**

- Choose a free voice recorder app that provides a waveform of the speech being recorded. There are a number of these available online, such as Rev Recorder or Wavepad. Download the app onto your phone and/or tablet and get your students to do the same.
- To begin using the app, choose two- or three-syllable words like *London*, *doctor*, *beautiful*, or *decorate*. Choose words that your students regularly stress wrongly.

✓ *Getting it right*   The best time to get your students to practise word stress is when you present new vocabulary. However, even after an initial practice session, you may notice that some students are repeatedly misplacing the stress on certain words. This activity is ideal for words like these that have proven resistant to earlier attempts to learn correct stress.

- Using one of your target words, tell students that you are going to pronounce it with both correct and incorrect word stress. Do this and ask them to say which version was correct. Now do it again with the same word, but this time project the image of the waveform onto the class screen at the same time. The difference in the waveforms for LONdon and lonDON, for example, should be obvious to your students. In the image below, made using Wavepad, the first waveform is for LONdon. The stress on the first syllable is clearly visible when we compare the image with that on the right, where the stress is on the second syllable (i.e. lonDON).

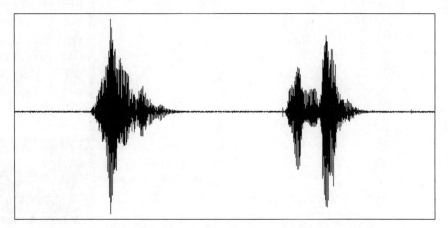

FIGURE 6.1.   *Waveforms showing the word 'London' pronounced correctly, with the stress on the first syllable (left) and incorrectly, with the stress on the second syllable (right)*

- Now invite your students to record themselves on their phones or tablets saying *London* with both correct and incorrect stress. The waveforms that they produce with the apps on their phones should look like yours. With a bit of practice, the students should be able to pronounce *London* with the correct stress.
- Next, put up the images of the waveforms for the correct pronunciation of the remaining words in the exercise, and invite your students to try to record only the correct versions of the words on their devices. Remind them to use the waveforms on the class screen to help them evaluate their attempts.

- In a later class, repeat these steps, but using short sentences or questions that your students regularly pronounce with incorrect sentence stress. An example of such a question is *What time is it?* which some students erroneously pronounce with the stress on *it* instead of *time*. The left-hand waveform below shows incorrect sentence stress, with *what, time,* and *it* fairly evenly stressed, as opposed to the correct sentence stress on the right, with *time* receiving most stress, *what* receiving some stress, and *is* and *it* receiving the least.

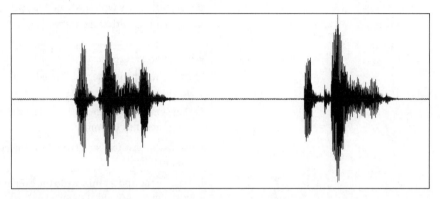

FIGURE 6.2. *Waveforms showing 'What time is it?' pronounced with incorrect stress (left) and correct stress (right)*

Why this works ▥▶ There are two clear advantages to using voice recording technology that is able to produce waveforms. The first is that when compared with the waveform for correct stress, the student's waveform provides them with a visual image of the level of accuracy of what they have just pronounced. This waveform offers the learner a complementary channel of input to their sense of hearing. The second advantage, particularly for students with access to an app on their own phone or tablet, is that they receive instant, individualized feedback on their attempts. This immediate feedback will motivate them to try again if they see that their previous attempt is wrong.

Evaluating apps and other pronunciation software

New technology is not necessarily good technology, and technology aimed at teaching and learning pronunciation is no exception. A lot of apps look like they are going to do a good job of helping learners, but on closer inspection turn out to have significant limitations. As teachers, we need to have a clear idea of which factors make an app good or not. We then need to be able to show our students how to identify an effective learning tool so that they can go and find the apps that best suit their own goals.

Try this ☞ **The best app for me**
- Ask your students if they know of any pronunciation apps, either for use online or for smartphone, tablet, or desktop computer. If they do, give two or three students time to tell the whole class which apps they know about or have used. Encourage them to say what they like and don't like about each app.

- Next, using a projector and your class computer, do an internet search for pronunciation apps. The words 'English pronunciation apps' will generate a lot of hits, often referring users to the 'best' or 'top' apps. Ask the class what they think will make a 'top' pronunciation app. Accept all suggestions, making a note of each one on the class board.
- Now project a slide of Table 6.1 onto the class screen. The questions are those that learners should be asking themselves when they try out an app. The criteria are the standards by which you can judge a pronunciation app. Ask students to match the questions with the criteria.

Questions	Criteria
1. Does the app give me what I need? Can I choose what I want to work on?	a) Cost
2. Can I choose the order in which I do the exercises and the speed at which I advance?	b) Feedback
3. Is the app easy to install? Are the instructions for the exercises easy to follow?	c) Progress
4. Is there the opportunity to do the exercises again and again until I'm really good at them?	d) Repetition
5. Does the app tell me immediately if I am right or wrong? If I am wrong, does the app show me how to change my pronunciation? Or do I just get an emoji?	e) Sequence and pace
6. Does the app keep a record of all of my exercises so that I can easily see if I am getting better?	f) Suitability and choice
7. Is the app free? If not, does it cost a lot? Is it easy to pay for?	g) User-friendliness

TABLE 6.1. *Matching activity: questions and criteria for identifying a good pronunciation app*

- When you can see that the class is finishing the activity, either give them the answers directly or invite the class to give them. (1–f / 2–e / 3–g / 4–d / 5–b / 6–c / 7–a). Compare the factors for 'top' apps (i.e. the criteria) with those that your students suggested earlier. Comment on any points where they coincide and invite the students to use all of the ideas from the class to make their own list of key criteria to consider when choosing an app for pronunciation.
- OPTIONAL: Ask students to each find two apps, and to report back on them using the criteria from this activity.

Why this works ▐▐▶

The increasing number of pronunciation apps available means that learners need some simple criteria to allow them to choose the right app. No single app will fulfil all the criteria that come out of this activity, but having their own list will help students to be more selective in the apps they finally decide to use. Combining their own suggestions with the seven criteria in the table means that each learner has their own individualized list, which in turn means that they are more likely to use them when looking for a good pronunciation app.

7 Listening and accommodation

Wherever English is used as an international language, users are exposed to a wide range of different accents. These accents are the natural outcome of English being used so extensively around the world, and we need to raise our students' awareness of this so that they understand that:

- accents are a natural and desirable feature of the use of English today;
- the continued use of English for international communication will give rise to yet more accents;
- users of English need to be able to understand different accents, and to learn how to adjust their own accent, if necessary, to help their listeners.

Learners who use English in an environment that is rich in different accents, such as a major world city, will, almost subconsciously, become accustomed to adjusting (or accommodating) their listening to the accents they encounter. But for many learners around the world, the reality is that they mostly hear English spoken with the accent that is typical of their home country and, in particular, of their classmates. As teachers, we need to help these learners to improve their ability to deal with English spoken in other accents. That is to say, they need to work on the skills of receptive phonological **accommodation**. To help them with this, we need to carefully introduce them to a range of different accents through activities that push them to explore the particular features of these accents.

A higher-level skill is the ability to adjust your own pronunciation to make yourself easier to understand for a listener who is not familiar with your accent, or who has limited receptive accommodation skills. This ability to adjust your pronunciation is known as productive phonological accommodation, and is best acquired using English for international communication. But it can also be practised in class in preparation for the real-life use of English.

Raising awareness of accents of English

Although accents are the norm for all languages, learners often come to class with the notion that only one accent of English is correct, and that although others exist, they are not really acceptable. As a major step towards our students using English for international communication, we need to help them see that this notion of a single correct accent is not true.

Try this ☞ **Getting comfortable with accents**

- Start by asking your students to make a list of the accents that are typical of their first language. On the class board or screen, make a note of the different accents they suggest.

- Put the class into small groups. Invite individual students to tell the group if they have a preferred accent and why, and if there is an accent they dislike, and why.

 *Getting it right*

> In classes where the students share the same L1, it doesn't matter how you form these groups. In a class with students from very different L1s, try to form groups composed of students with different first languages.

- If the country the students are from has a recognized standard accent, encourage them to say how they feel about this accent and why they think it became the standard.
- Ask students to discuss what they would do if they moved to an area of their home country that had a different accent from their own. Would they keep their own accent, or would they try to imitate the new local accent?
- Next, ask your students how they would feel if they were obliged to speak their first language in an accent other than the one that they naturally use. Encourage them to reflect on what impact it would have on them if they were forbidden to use their natural accent with their family and their friends.
- Finally, bring the whole class together and go back through the points they have discussed in groups, inviting individual students to make their comments to the whole class.

 *Getting it right*

> Guide this discussion, especially the whole-class discussion, tactfully. Point out that accents are completely natural in all languages, noting that they often indicate where we are from, and so are a part of our personal identity. Suggest that our reactions to accents are very often more emotional than rational, and that this can bring about prejudices. Finally, make it clear that where English is being used for international communication, we can speak it with any accent we choose, provided we are intelligible to our listeners.

Why this works ▶

> In many parts of the world, accents are bound up with all sorts of social prejudices, with one accent usually being given more prestige than other accents in the same country. This is especially true for English, and learners sometimes share this belief. However, by getting them to discuss accents related to their mother tongue, we can encourage them to reflect on their real-life experience. These reflections will lead them towards a greater understanding, tolerance, and respect for the different accents that they will encounter when using English as an international language.

Accommodating to different accents as a listener

Once learners are open to the notion of accent variation through an activity like the last one (or 'Accents online' in Chapter 6), we need to help them to deal with different accents more effectively. Fortunately, research shows that exposure to a range of accents makes listeners better at understanding both the accents we introduce them to explicitly in the classroom and other accents that are new to them.

Try this  **Exploring accents**

This activity pushes learners towards some very simple accent exploration. To allow them to focus on the pronunciation, it is best to do the activity with a scripted text that they can read before listening to the accents.

- Find a scripted text that is available in different accents. Suitable texts can be found online at IDEA (the International Dialects of English Archive – see Appendix 4), the Speech Accent Archive (see Appendix 4), or in the recordings that accompany *Teaching the Pronunciation of English as a Lingua Franca* (see 'Recommended reading' in Appendix 3).
- Ask the students to read the script. Check that they understand it, helping where necessary.
- Invite your students to read the text aloud to their partners.
- Play the recording of the first accent you have chosen. The students listen to the speaker's accent and try to place it on a world map or say where the speaker is from.

✓ *Getting it right*

This mapping exercise can be quite hard, but it is a fun task that focuses the students' attention on the accents, as opposed to the content, which they are already familiar with. If they are struggling to identify the accents, give them two or three options to choose from for each recording.

- Play each recording again, and invite students to comment on anything that they find different or interesting about each speaker's accent.
- Finally, ask the class what they imagine listeners to their own accent of English are most likely to perceive as being different or interesting.

Why this works ▷▷▷

In the activity 'A window on the world' in Chapter 6, we simply exposed students to different accents without focusing on what made each accent the way it is. This activity encourages learners to explore features of different accents at a very simple level. Nevertheless, even this simple highlighting of what sounds different or interesting is a start in making a learner a more flexible listener, and so improving their receptive phonological accommodation skills.

The next level in equipping students to deal with accent variation is to get them to focus on specific features across various English accents. These could be features where variation is not problematic for intelligibility. The different ways in which speakers pronounce *th* or the letter *r* fit into this category, as do the different qualities of the vowels of different accents. Alternatively, you could focus on areas that are key for intelligibility, but that your students find hard to pronounce, such as particular consonants, word-initial consonant clusters, vowel length, or sentence stress.

Try this  **Targeting specific features**

- Choose a specific feature of pronunciation to focus on, and then use resources such as IDEA, ELLLO, Dynamic Dialects, the Speech Accent Archive, or *Teaching the Pronunciation of English as a Lingua Franca* to find a speaker whose accent exemplifies your target feature. The first time you do this activity, the accent you choose could be that of speakers from neighbouring countries, or from a country that your students have regular contact with.

- Give your students the usual pre-listening background information and set them some simple comprehension questions.
- Play the recording. Then check their understanding by going over their answers to the comprehension questions.

 **Getting it right**

With unscripted recordings, it is important that your students are happy that they have mostly understood the speaker before moving on to the focus on the target feature. If necessary, play the recording more than once until they are comfortable with the content.

- Now introduce the class to the target pronunciation feature. If it is the *th* in words like *the*, *that*, or *then*, for example, make this clear, and ask them how the *th* in these words is pronounced in an online dictionary, or by most native speakers.
- Play the recording again, encouraging your students to listen out for the target feature and, in particular, for how the speaker pronounces it. If the target feature is the pronunciation of *th*, this will often be like /d/, making *de*, *dat*, and *den*, or it might be like /z/, making *ze*, *zat*, and *zen*.
- Repeat the recording if asked to, and then invite the students to discuss what they heard, first with their partner, and then with the whole class.
- Repeat the activity at regular intervals with a different feature and accent each time.

Why this works ⫸

Repeated, guided exposure to specific features across a range of accents leads to greater familiarity with them. This gradually leads to improved receptive phonological accommodation skills. Repeating the activity will not only benefit students' listening skills, but also increase their understanding and tolerance of accent diversity in English as an international language.

Try this ☞ **Listen and transcribe**

- Find a recording of a speaker with a non-native-speaker accent that your students are unfamiliar with. Select a short piece of the recording (less than one minute) for the activity.
- Tell your students the first-language background of the speaker and any other biodata that might be of interest, such as the speaker's age and profession.
- Play the recording once and ask the students what it was about in general.
- Play it again and ask for anything else that they have understood.
- Now tell the class that they have to write down, word for word, what the speaker says. Invite them to work in pairs if they want to.
- Play very short sections of the recording (about five seconds at a time), replaying each section two or three times if requested to do so, and allowing the students time to write between each playing.
- Finish by playing the whole recording one more time. Allow students time to make any final changes or additions. Then show them the full transcript.
- After the students have had time to compare the transcript with what they have written, explore any features of the speaker's pronunciation that they found difficult to transcribe.

Why this works ▐▐▐▶ | Although this is not an easy activity, and is similar in some ways to a dictation, transcription is a very good measure of intelligibility. In addition, in this activity (as opposed to in a dictation), analysing the parts of the recording that your students weren't able to transcribe successfully brings about learning, rather than failure. Often, these problem sections relate to features of the speaker's accent, and their detailed examination helps to improve your students' receptive accommodation skills.

Accommodating your pronunciation to your listener

If receptive phonological accommodation allows our students to adjust their expectations as listeners, then productive phonological accommodation allows them to adjust their output in order to make it easier for listeners to understand them. With groups where the learners come from a variety of L1 backgrounds, communication activities such as quizzes, information gap, problem-solving, or discussions offer a natural environment for these adjustments to occur. Such accommodations will gradually cause the various speakers' pronunciation to converge on an internationally intelligible accent. This process is summarized in Figure 7.1.

| The desire to communicate pushes the speakers to converge on a common pronunciation. | → | The convergence on the common pronunciation leads to the replacement of problematic pronunciation features by internationally intelligible features. | → | The L1 influence in the speaker's accent decreases, leading to increased international intelligibility. |

FIGURE 7.1. *Mixed-L1 classes: convergence on internationally intelligible pronunciation*

Try this  **Making yourself understood (mixed-L1 classes only)**

- Choose a suitable communication activity for your group. This will preferably be one from their coursebook, and should be of a type that they are already familiar with.
- Set the activity up as you normally would. Just before telling the students to start, ask them what they can do during the activity if they don't understand a word or phrase that a speaker has said. Hopefully, their suggestions will include basic requests for help such as:
  - ♦ Sorry? / I'm sorry?
  - ♦ [Unintelligible word]? (i.e. the listener repeats the word/phrase that they haven't understood as best they can.)
  - ♦ I don't understand [unintelligible word]. / What is [unintelligible word]?

✓ **Getting it right** | Some students can be reluctant to make requests for repetition. Assure them that it is natural for speakers not to understand each other from time to time, and that the best way to deal with this situation is to ask the speaker to repeat the problematic word or phrase.

- Set the activity going, and go around observing progress and congratulating any instances of requests for repetition and successful repair.
- When the communication activity is over, invite different pairs or groups to tell the class about an incident that occurred during the activity where they managed successful repair.

One issue with communication activities carried out between students who share an L1 is that the desire to communicate drives the speakers to adjust their pronunciation towards what is common for them. This usually leads to increased local intelligibility (i.e. in the classroom) at the cost of reduced international intelligibility, as we see in Figure 7.2.

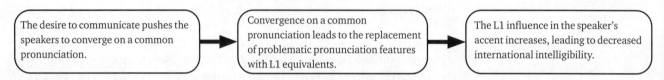

FIGURE 7.2.   *Shared-L1 classes: convergence on shared-L1 pronunciation and loss of international intelligibility*

One way of providing learners in a shared L1 environment with practice in deliberately modifying their pronunciation so as to achieve international intelligibility is the use of student recordings (see Chapter 6). Ask learners to record a text, and then reward marks for the correct pronunciation of target features (chosen from the features that are key for international intelligibility – see Appendix 1). In this way, learners are motivated to modify their accent in the direction that will make them intelligible and get them good marks.

A simpler, but effective and entertaining way to offer learners the chance to accommodate productively is through games such as Mark Hancock's *Pronunciation Journey*. The game is a variation on traditional minimal-pair discrimination exercises, but the listeners' decisions on hearing one or other word from a minimal pair will take them left or right at each of four junctions. The sample in Figure 7.3 was designed for Brazilian learners of English, who often add a slight vowel sound after a final consonant, so that, for example, *cough* sounds like *coffee*. In this case, they hear the following sequence: (1) *cough*, (2) *coffee*, (3) *coffee*, (4) *cough*, and are taken to Cape Town.

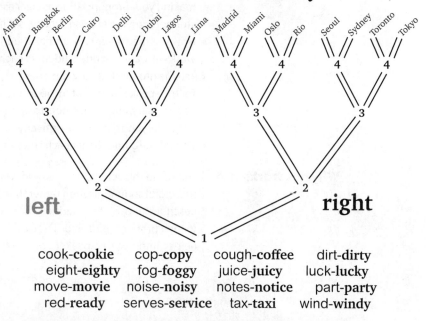

Pronunciation Journey

left	right

cook-**cookie**   cop-**copy**   cough-**coffee**   dirt-**dirty**
eight-**eighty**   fog-**foggy**   juice-**juicy**   luck-**lucky**
move-**movie**   noise-**noisy**   notes-**notice**   part-**party**
red-**ready**   serves-**service**   tax-**taxi**   wind-**windy**

FIGURE 7.3. Pronunciation Journey *for Brazilian speakers of English (first published in the newsletter of the IATEFL Pronunciation SIG). Hancock, M. (2013). Accommodation games 2.* Speak Out!, *48, 30–31*

Traditionally, the speaker in this type of game is the teacher, and so it is assumed that any errors are on the part of the listeners. However, Mark has repurposed the activity so that it has become an exercise in productive accommodation by getting the students to read the words aloud and allowing the listeners to signal that they need the speaker to repeat a given word.

Try this ☞ **Let me try again (shared-L1 classes)**

- Set up a *Pronunciation Journey* map using two words or phrases that are regularly confused by your learners because of problems related to their first-language pronunciation.
- Tell the students how the game works. Play it once as a demonstration, with you saying the words, and your students acting as listeners.
- Play the game again. If the students arrive at the right city, congratulate them. If they end up at the wrong city, ask them to think about why this might have happened.

✓ Getting it right   Normally, students will assume that they arrived at the wrong city as a result of poor discrimination as listeners. Explain to them that in a world with so many different accents of English, the problem can be as much the speaker's as the listener's, and that good speakers will actively adjust their pronunciation until they are understood.

- Repeat the game with the same pair of words/phrases in the same sequence, making your pronunciation as clear as possible. This should get most of the students arriving at the right city, but if not, repeat once more.
- Now put the students into small groups. Give the class a suitable minimal pair to work with, and get one student in each group to prepare a pronunciation journey.
- Tell the groups that they can now carry out their own journeys. Stress the need for the speaker to repeat the journey, making adjustments to their pronunciation as necessary, and for listeners to openly request help (as in the previous activity), until everyone gets to the right city.
- Repeat the game so that each student has the chance to be the speaker.

Why this works ⏵ The key to this activity is the way in which it foregrounds working towards successful communication rather than listeners being 'wrong'. Done in the way described above, the onus is on the speaker to make deliberate adjustments to their pronunciation in order to achieve successful communication. This will help to improve the speaker's productive accommodation skills.

8 When a native-speaker accent is the goal

As we have seen in previous chapters, international intelligibility is a suitable learning objective to work towards for most learners of English. However, there are various personal reasons why a student may wish to work towards a goal of native-like English instead: they might want to live in, and integrate into, a native-speaker community and they feel that speaking in the same way will help them to fit in; it could be for a job, such as acting or performing, in which a certain accent may be important; or it may even be because they want to speak like a famous person they know and like. It is our job as teachers to offer support and constructive advice to students on how they can meet their language goals, whatever they may be.

Which native-speaker accent?

If students are certain they wish to work towards a native-speaker accent, the next step is for them to narrow down which accent it is that they want to produce. Due to the prevalence of two prestige native-speaker English accents throughout ELT materials and media – Standard Southern British English, also known as Received Pronunciation (RP), and **General American** (GA) – students may incorrectly believe that these are their only options. It is important to clarify this, informing them that there is a huge range of English accents from all over the world that they can choose from, not just RP and GA. Additionally, the fact that students are familiar with these accents due to hearing them so frequently does not necessarily mean that they will be easy for them to produce; they may instead discover through the following activities that there are other accents which are far less challenging to acquire.

Try this 👉 **Raising students' awareness of the diversity of accent models**

- Inform students that they are going to do some research into different native English accents; their goal is to listen to a range of recordings and find one they like and would be happy to produce.
- Provide students with links to a variety of online resources such as the YouTube channel Accent Base, the Speech Accent Archive, YouGlish, Dynamic Dialects, or any other site where they can listen to a range of native-speaker English accents.
- Instruct students to spend some time exploring these resources, listening to speakers from several English-speaking locations, making notes about where each speaker is from and what they liked or disliked about their pronunciation.

- Once students have settled on a pronunciation they like, they should do a little more research on it. This could include general information, such as where it is spoken, how many people speak this way (if known), and any famous people who have this accent. They could also look for more specific information on its features, noting down their findings and some example words and pronunciations to bring to their next class.
- Invite students to share their findings with a partner or group, and then, if appropriate, with the rest of the class.

 **✓ Getting it right**

> If students need a more structured approach and clearer guidance to begin this task, encourage them to start by researching the particular vowels and consonants that they find most difficult to pronounce. They could cross-check vowel sounds using the accents chart on the Dynamic Dialects website, listening, and then comparing their pronunciation with that of speakers from different parts of the world. Alternatively, they could type words or phrases containing challenging consonant sounds into the YouGlish website, and listen to the ways in which speakers from different parts of the world produce them.

Accent role models

One way of helping students to engage with their chosen accent goal is to ask them to find an accent role model. This should be a native speaker they like, who is in the public eye with accessible media recordings, and who has the accent that the student wishes to emulate. The goal of this activity is for students to study this person speaking and, over a period of time, to try to adopt their accent, and even their speech style.

Try this ☞ **Asking students to find their own accent role model**

- Ask students to share with the class the names of some famous native speakers of English that they know of, such as actors, musicians, sports stars, or politicians. Ask them if they would like to speak English in a similar way, and if so, why.
- Tell your students that for homework, you want them to find their own accent role model – a speaker of English as a first language whom they like and would be happy to emulate. To do this, they should watch or listen to English language media, such as TV programmes (dramas, soaps, and documentaries), movies, political speeches, TED talks, or podcasts.
- Once they have identified a role model, students should aim to listen to at least 20 minutes of their speech, and observe their pronunciation of certain sounds. For instance, they might start by focusing on consonants, such as:
  - ♦ the voiced and unvoiced dental fricatives /ð/ and /θ/ (represented in written words by *th*): Do they pronounce them? If they don't, what sounds do they use instead? Do they perhaps use /f/, /t/, /d/, or /v/?
  - ♦ **connected speech:** what examples of consonant–vowel linking do they use in their speech?
  - ♦ the /r/ sound: how and when do they pronounce it? Do they pronounce it wherever it appears, or only before vowels?
  - ♦ the /t/ sound: how do they pronounce it? Is it always a /t/ sound? Or is it sometimes pronounced more like a /d/? Does the /t/ ever disappear completely?

- Give students a week to practise copying their speaker's pronunciation and speech style at home, using their notes and recordings to help them.
- On the day that you have assigned, students share their accent model research and some example pronunciations with their peers.
- As an ongoing project, students should continue to follow their accent model over time, revisiting their recordings, and finding and watching new ones.

 **Getting it right**

To benefit from this activity, it is important that students choose an accent role model they like and feel comfortable emulating. However, even if they have chosen their accent model carefully, they may at first feel uncomfortable or embarrassed about replicating their pronunciation and speech style. To overcome this, provide them with plenty of time to practise from the privacy of home until they feel confident enough to share their progress and learning with their classmates.

Why this works ▶

Insisting that students pronounce English in a way that they actively dislike or feel no personal connection to can be demotivating and inhibiting, and could result in reduced participation during class time. However, including activities that are personalized to their own pronunciation goals, encouraging them to consider how they would like to sound when speaking English, and picturing their future selves as a proficient speaker of their chosen accent can be very motivating. Even if your students have differing goals, this activity is flexible enough to be used with any target-accent role model, whether the model is a native speaker or a proficient non-native speaker.

Meeting the goals of a divided classroom

It may become clear that there is a divide in the classroom between students wanting to work towards a native-speaker accent and those who don't. One way in which teachers can satisfy all learners is to suggest a syllabus which balances both goals, dividing lessons into productive and receptive content. For productive learning, draw from the features of the Lingua Franca Core (LFC). The common features between the LFC and native-speaker accents ensure plenty of overlap which will suit all learners.

When it comes to the more specific native-speaker features, such as connected speech and weak vowels, include them in class, but clarify to students that they have a choice as to how they go on to use them. For those who are working towards international intelligibility, the lesson content can be taken as practice in 'pronunciation for listening'; this will help them to identify and understand these features when heard in native-speaker speech.

Try this ☞ **Using a dictogloss to provide productive and receptive practice**

A dictogloss activity can be a useful way to highlight features common to native speakers such as **vowel weakening** and connected speech; it's also an effective method of demonstrating the impact these features can have on listeners. While traditionally, these activities are read aloud by the teacher, in this modified exercise, you use an audio recording from a recent classroom listening activity containing authentic native-speaker speech. Students listen to several sentences from the recording, and when each one is finished, they try to write down what they remember hearing. To complete the task, students compare answers in pairs or groups and try to reconstruct a final version of what they heard, relying on their collective notes and memories.

- Take a recent listening activity you have used with your students, locating five short sections within it containing the pronunciation features you want to draw students' attention to, such as connected speech or weakened vowels.
- Make a note of where in the recording these sections begin and end. This will allow you to easily navigate between them.
- Once in class, ask students a few questions about the recording. Ask them to summarize what they remember of it to refresh their memory of the topic and prepare them for the activity.
- Tell the students that they will now hear several short clips taken from their listening activity. While each clip plays, they should do nothing except listen carefully and try to remember what they heard.
- Play the recordings. When each has finished, ask students to write down what they can remember.
- When all the clips have been played, put students into pairs or groups. They compare their notes and try to decide on a final correct transcription.
- Provide students with the model texts. These can be written or projected onto the board. Students then compare what they wrote with the model.

✓ *Getting it right*   The main objective of this exercise is to expose students to the features commonly used by native speakers, allowing them to discover how sounds change and merge together when spoken at a natural pace. To facilitate this, allow the students to listen as many times as they need to. Upload the audio files to an accessible online folder so that they can be revisited at home after the lesson.

Focusing on function words

Dictogloss activities are a useful way to identify the specific difficulties your students may be having understanding native-speaker speech. Once you have established exactly which features are causing them to struggle, such as connected speech or vowel weakening in function words, you can target those, picking them out of any listening content you work on in class, and using them for short, spontaneous listening practices.

Try this    **Following up on function words**

- Select the phrases (or 'chunks') you want to use; take these from a recent listening activity which students are familiar with and which contain authentic speech. Ensure your phrases contain several function words, as in Figure 8.1, as these will most likely have consonant–vowel, consonant–consonant, or vowel–vowel connections and vowel weakening.

Example 1: 'you're in a ...'. This phrase often becomes 'yourina' /jərɪnə/ due to:

♦ unstressed vowels weakening to **schwa**;

♦ consonant–vowel linking between the final /r/ of *your* and the initial /ɪ/ of *in*;

♦ consonant–vowel linking between the final /n/ of *in* and the following schwa.

'you're in a'

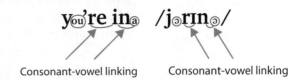

Consonant-vowel linking   Consonant-vowel linking

Vowels reduced to schwa /ə/

FIGURE 8.1.   *How 'you're in a' can sound when said in naturally occurring speech*

Example 2: 'a little bit about'. If used in naturally occurring speech, this can become 'a little bitabout' or /əlɪtlbɪtəbaʊt/ due to:
- ♦ vowels weakening to schwa
- ♦ consonant–vowel linking between /t/ in *bit* and /ə/ in *about*.

'a little bit about'

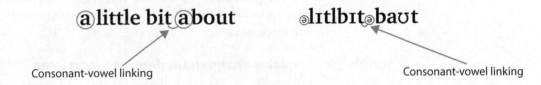

Consonant-vowel linking   Consonant-vowel linking

Vowels reduced to schwa /ə/

FIGURE 8.2.   *How the phrase 'a little bit about' can sound when said in naturally occurring speech*

- Remind students of the listening source your chosen phrases have come from by asking them to summarize what they remember from it, its key points, or if they liked/disliked it and why.
- Tell them they will hear some short phrases from this source and they should listen and try to identify what's been said.
- Play the phrases several times and ask students to just listen and try to understand.
- Invite the class to compare what they think they have heard with a partner and write down the phrase they both agree on.
- Invite students to share what they heard. Write the correct answer on the board.
- Play the recording again and trace your finger over the sounds as they are spoken aloud, allowing students to listen and notice each connection and just how short the weakened vowels can become.
- Elicit from them the features they noticed, annotating the phrase on the board as in Figures 8.1 and 8.2, documenting it as it was actually spoken.
- Ask students to practise chanting the phrase aloud with you at natural speed several times.

Getting it right

At first, students may find this activity challenging. They might describe the phrases containing function words as sounding like one long word with no clear breaks between them. Annotating the phrase on the board and providing a visual representation of what they are hearing is therefore important. It's also a helpful reminder that students can copy down and take away with them, using it to practise the phrases on their own after class.

Some final choral practice is a helpful way to get students used to producing connected speech and weakened vowel sounds, which at first may feel very strange compared to their usual way of pronouncing the sounds. By practising from within the safety of a group, students don't have to worry about making mistakes, they can simply focus on getting comfortable with the sounds, the speed, and the rhythm.

Reproducing native-speaker speech from authentic resources

Once your students have had time to practise hearing, identifying, and producing function words in classroom materials, increase the challenge by providing them with longer excerpts from authentic resources featuring native speakers.

Try this ☞ **Preparing a script and performing a short scene**

In this activity, students take their experience of decoding and use it to predict how native speakers will pronounce certain words (stressed or unstressed, linking or not, reduced or in their full form). They then listen to check if their predictions are correct, and practise reproducing the language in full, rehearsing and then performing the scene.

- Identify a dialogue from an audio or video recording that your students would find interesting and relevant.
- Locate or produce a transcript of this scene, writing down every word in full that the speakers say. Ensure that you have a link or recording of the scene you can take to class and play.
- Put students into pairs or small groups and ask them to work together, reading the transcript and identifying any places where they think a vowel might be weakened (such as in function words), or where a link might appear. (This could be a consonant–consonant, consonant–vowel, or vowel–vowel link).
- Play the recording for students. They listen to the speaker and put a tick or a cross above the relevant section of the script to indicate whether their prediction was correct or incorrect.
- Once the recording has finished, project the script onto the board and invite the groups to come up to the board and annotate the script to show exactly how the speaker said the words.
- Inform students that they are now going to reproduce or perform the excerpt with their group for the class. They should spend some time rehearsing together, emulating the native speakers' pronunciations, and giving each other feedback.
- Students perform the scene for the class, attempting to reproduce the speech as the speakers did.

 **Getting it right**

Incorporating students' target accent models into this activity can be very motivating for them, particularly when the production stages of the task are reached. To make it even more student-centred and creative, invite the class to choose and source their own scenes, which could be performed live or recorded, with students getting peer or teacher feedback. Alternatively, if you are using a video recording, students could dub their audio performance over the original scene, replacing the speakers. Using relatable real-life media, humorous scenes, or speakers from a similar age range, peer group, or background to your students can be an effective way to increase their engagement with this activity.

9 Integration

With everything else that we are required to do in class, pronunciation can easily get pushed aside; it is almost as though it does not have the same importance as grammar, vocabulary, or the four skills. But two things should cause us to stop and think about this, and to remedy it as best we can. The first is that surveys repeatedly reveal pronunciation to be high on the list of what learners think is important. The second is that rather than being an add-on, pronunciation is actually central to learning English. It is like a base-level 'program' that works quietly away in the background while the other language systems – vocabulary, speaking, and so on – are in operation. As with any base-level system, if you take it away, the rest of the system will operate badly, or not at all.

If a student struggles to get words out because they are unsure about their pronunciation, their confidence as a speaker is likely to diminish over time. And if they do not know how words are pronounced, it can be very difficult to identify them in the speech of others. But the connection between pronunciation and the skills of speaking and listening is not the end of the story. We know from research that learners from a great many first-language backgrounds need to know how to pronounce the words they are seeing on the page so as to be able to process them efficiently, either to learn vocabulary or to make sense of what they are reading.

Pronunciation is not an optional extra that we add on if we have time. It is the very glue that holds the systems of the English language together. And this means that we need to integrate the work we do on pronunciation into work on vocabulary and grammar, as well as into work on the skills of speaking, listening, and reading.

Pronunciation, speaking, and listening

The link between pronunciation and speaking and listening skills is clear to teachers and learners alike, so it makes sense to begin integrating pronunciation practice into speaking and listening activities first.

Try this ☞ **Do you know how to pronounce this?**
- Lead into a speaking activity from the class coursebook in your usual way. When you are working on the vocabulary for the activity, invite your students to go through any key words and phrases looking for potential pronunciation problems.
- Encourage students to seek help from a classmate if they encounter any problems ('Do you know how to pronounce this?') before asking you to help.

 **Getting it right** | Getting students to seek help from their peers is part of making them increasingly independent learners. Encourage them to use dictionaries (printed or online) in class to check their pronunciation.

- Run the speaking activity. While the students are working, go around the class checking on any pronunciation issues that came up during the lead-in. Make a note of any that still require attention. Alternatively, ask students to note down any problems they had. Then, using their notes, you can create a group-specific follow-up pronunciation activity focusing on these problems.

Why this works ▌▌▌▶ | Establishing the pronunciation of key vocabulary items before or while speaking satisfies an immediate and obvious need that individual students or a whole class has. This 'here and now' work is more effective than pronunciation work done in isolation from the rest of learning English.

Try this ☞ **Before we listen**

Just as with speaking, it is important that students deal with any major pronunciation problems they have before any listening tasks they have to do.

- As you prepare a listening activity, check the audio script and pick out any vocabulary that your students might not know how to pronounce.
- During the lead-in to the listening activity, pre-teach the key vocabulary – its meaning and its pronunciation.
- Play the recording for the first time, but tell the class not to worry about the comprehension questions yet. Ask them instead to raise a hand each time they hear one of the words whose pronunciation they have just practised.

 **Getting it right** | This first listening focuses specifically on pronunciation, but it is also useful in that it gives the students a chance to 'tune in' to the voices and accents of the speakers in the recording.

- Continue with your normal procedure for listening practice, with the students carrying out the listening tasks in their coursebook.

Why this works ▌▌▌▶ | Pronunciation problems can impact heavily on understanding when listening. The word *Asia*, for example, is pronounced /ˈasia/ in Spanish and /ˈazja/ in Italian, with none of the sounds coinciding with the sounds of the English pronunciation. As a result, students expecting /ˈasia/ or /ˈazja/ do not identify /ˈeɪʒə/ as being the same word. Moreover, the unintelligible sounds that they do hear distract them, causing them to miss out on what comes next.

Try this ☞ **Was there anything you didn't understand?**

As a complement to pre-listening pronunciation work, it can be useful to do some post-listening work once all the comprehension questions have been answered.

- Work through the listening task, playing the recording and checking the answers with the class in the usual way.
- On checking the answers, your students are likely to mention one or two short sections that they found unintelligible. If necessary, play the recording again and ask the students to stop you when they get to one of the problem sections.
- Focus the students' attention on the problematic section. Play it two or three times and ask them to suggest what the words might be.

- If they still cannot decode the problem section, you can either pronounce it for them yourself more slowly than in the recording, or you can invite the students to find the section in the script for the recording at the back of the coursebook.
- Next, play the problematic section while they read it in the coursebook.
- Finally, invite students to comment on what they have noticed in the speaker's pronunciation. Guide them towards focusing on any unusual pronunciation of individual sounds as well as connected speech issues such as weak forms, etc.

Pronunciation, vocabulary, and reading

When we read words on a page or screen, we silently pronounce these words to ourselves in our head. We do this to move the words around what is called the phonological loop, a part of the brain that processes words we read so that they can be sent off to our long-term memory for storage, or for comparison with words already stored in the long-term memory. However, if we don't know a word's pronunciation, this processing can fail, and consequently nothing gets sent to the long-term memory. As a result, the reader cannot remember what they have just read. For the same reason, if a learner can't pronounce an item of the vocabulary they are trying to learn, they will very quickly forget it since it won't be sent to the long-term memory. This doesn't mean that learners have to be able to pronounce new vocabulary like a native speaker; however, it does mean that they have to have a stable pronunciation of all new vocabulary. This stable pronunciation will be:

- easy for them to pronounce;
- intelligible to their listeners, both native and non-native speakers.

Try this ☞ **I know this word. Or do I?**

- Before looking at some new vocabulary, ask students what they mean when they say 'I know this word'. Get them to suggest what aspects of a word they are referring to when they say they know it.
- Praise students for answers that refer to a word's spelling, its meaning, its translation in the students' first language, its grammatical category (noun, verb, adjective, etc.), synonyms, and so on.
- If nobody suggests it, add 'pronunciation' yourself, and explain to the class that if you don't know a word's pronunciation, this will impact negatively when you try to use it, even if you know all the other aspects.
- Explain that when you can't pronounce a word:
  - ♦ you won't recognize it when you are listening to someone who uses it when speaking;
  - ♦ people probably won't recognize the word when you pronounce it;
  - ♦ you will find it hard to memorize the word when you are learning vocabulary;
  - ♦ you will find it hard to remember the word when you are reading.
- Ask the students for any personal stories or anecdotes that they have that illustrate what you just said about vocabulary and pronunciation.
- Tell the whole class that from now on you expect them to include notes about pronunciation in any lists of new vocabulary.

Why this works ⫸

> By highlighting pronunciation as one of the top things you have to know when learning a new word or phrase, you significantly increase your students' awareness of its importance for learning and using English successfully. By asking your students for anecdotes, you connect pronunciation to their personal experience of using English. By asking them to include pronunciation notes in their vocabulary lists, you give them a simple, effective tool for remembering the pronunciation of new words.

Try this ☞ **Look at the spelling**

The spelling of English words seems chaotic to many learners, especially those whose first language has a one-to-one relationship between letters in the alphabet and their pronunciation. But there are a lot of simple letter–sound relationships in English, too, and these can help learners with the pronunciation of new vocabulary.

- Select vocabulary that your students have already come across in their coursebook and that is representative of the sound–spelling rule you want to present. For example, you could select words that represent the pronunciations of the letter *i* in words like *mine*, where the *i* is pronounced /aɪ/, and *his*, where it is pronounced /ɪ/.

✓ Getting it right

> Using vocabulary from units in your coursebook that you have already covered has the advantage that students are familiar with the meaning and are free to concentrate on the spelling and pronunciation.

- Write the words you have chosen in a random fashion on the class board or screen. Then put the students into pairs or small groups.
- Show the class two guide words. So, for example, if you want to work on the difference between /aɪ/ and /ɪ/, you might choose *mine* and *his* as guide words.
- Ask the class how they are pronounced, confirming correct pronunciation or modelling the pronunciation if necessary.
- Isolate the vowel sounds in the guide words, getting your students to pronounce both vowels once you have modelled them.
- Invite the students to work in their pairs/groups to classify the words on the board or screen as *mine* words or *his* words on the basis of the vowel sound for the letter *i*.
- Go round the class as your students are working, offering to pronounce any of the words that a pair or group is unsure of.
- Bring the whole class back together, and correct the task on the board or screen so that you end up with two lists of words, one under each guide word. See Figure 9.1 for *mine* and *his* lists.

mine	his
file	dictionary
flight	scissors
like	ticket
five	big
nine	rich
night	difficult
right	drink
time	listen
drive	windy
light	kitchen

FIGURE 9.1.　　*Lists of familiar words that represent a particular sound–spelling rule*

- Invite the class to look at the two lists and to propose a rule or rules for the spelling–sound relationship of the *mine* words, and another rule or rules for the *his* words.
- Guide the students' suggestions as necessary to draw the following conclusions:
  - ◆ *i* + consonant + final *e* = *mine* pronunciation
  - ◆ *ight* = *mine* pronunciation
  - ◆ *i* + final consonant = *his* pronunciation
  - ◆ *i* + two consonants = *his* pronunciation
- Ask the class if they know any other words that follow their new rules.
- Ask them if they know any words that do not follow these rules (for example *give*, *machine*, *find*, *mind*).

 **Getting it right**　　Although they can be frustrating, exceptions exist to all the rules of English sound–spelling relationships, and it is important to acknowledge this openly. It can even be fun to make a list of 'disobedient' spellings like *give* or *find*.

Why this works ▶　　A great deal of time and money has been spent on systems such as phonics that show young learners, both native and non-native, how to pronounce the words they see when they are reading. These systems strive to develop the regularities of the sound–spelling system of English, and are principally aimed at very young learners. But these same systems, adapted to the vocabulary that teenage and adult learners meet as they go through their coursebooks, will provide older learners with a powerful tool for guessing the pronunciation of new words, both while they are reading and as they are learning new vocabulary.

Try this ☞　　**Pre-reading pronunciation**

As with listening, it is important for learners to know most of the words in a text before they read it. Research has shown that if more than 10% of the vocabulary in a text is unknown, it is very difficult for learners to make sense of it. But as we saw earlier, knowing a word includes knowing its pronunciation.

- Before you do any reading tasks, tell your students to cast their eyes over the text and underline any words that they don't know how to pronounce.
- Next, invite individual students to come to the class board and write their words on it. Alternatively, ask students to write the problem words on small pieces of paper; then collect these in.

- Taking one word at a time, ask the class if anyone knows how to pronounce it.
- Praise correct attempts and get the whole class to repeat them. Alternatively, model the correct pronunciation yourself and have the class imitate you.
- Ask the students to carry out the reading task.

Try this  **Here is the news**

Asking students to read texts aloud that they have not previously studied is not recommended. The reader's attention will be split between trying to understand what they are saying and trying to pronounce words they are seeing for the first time. Quite a different matter is to get students to prepare a text for reading aloud in much the same way as a newsreader would for a radio or television news programme, or as many people do for podcasts and short informative videos on the internet.

- Explain to your students that they are going to prepare some texts for reading aloud. If possible, present the exercise as part of a wider project, with each student preparing part of a news bulletin for local radio, for example.

✓ *Getting it right*

Use texts that would normally be read aloud, for example, news items for TV and radio, weather forecasts, podcasts, scripted video commentaries, recipes, travel directions, plays, and poems. The key factor is that the text would, in 'real life', be prepared first, then rehearsed, and then read aloud.

- Give out the texts. For a small class, each student can have a different text. For a large class, choose five or six texts and distribute them evenly among students.
- Invite the students to work individually using their dictionaries or getting help from you or their classmates, in order to:
  1 understand the meaning of their text
  2 resolve any pronunciation problems they may have
  3 think about sentence stress for the text. (See Chapter 4 for more on this.)
- Give students time to rehearse reading out their texts. Move around the classroom and offer help where needed.
- Put the students into small groups so that each group has at least one person representing each of the texts.
- Invite one student in each group to read their text aloud to the other members of their group. The group members should give feedback on the speaker's overall intelligibility, and on any specific pronunciation problems the speaker had.
- Repeat the process until each person has had the chance to read aloud to the other members of their group.
- Finish by asking individual students to volunteer to read their text aloud to the whole class.

✓ *Getting it right*

Always seek volunteers for this last step, but if no one comes forward, choose one or two students who you know have good pronunciation. Then seek volunteers once more among the other students.

- If you wish, invite the students to record their texts for marking, and explain how the marks will contribute to their course evaluation. (See Chapter 6 for more on making recordings; see Chapter 10 for more on assessment.)

Why this works ▸

Preparing and reading a text aloud is one of the best ways of integrating pronunciation into an English lesson. To understand the text, students need to make sense of its grammar and vocabulary (although ideally, the text you use will not present much new language). If, in addition to recycling grammar and vocabulary, the text is then prepared for recording as part of a piece of project work, the whole exercise will have seamlessly integrated the following elements:

- recycling of known grammar and vocabulary items;
- practice in the pronunciation of individual sounds and words;
- practice in the pronunciation of whole phrases, especially correct pausing and sentence stress;
- practice in reading (and in writing if the students prepare their own texts);
- meaningful listening practice if the finished recordings are made available for other students to listen to.

Very few other activities can provide such strongly integrated pronunciation practice, and students generally find the activity highly motivating.

10   Assessing pronunciation

For most teachers, assessing pronunciation is not a stand-alone activity. Due to time constraints or lack of resources or knowledge, pronunciation assessment is frequently absorbed into student presentations and monologues. It can be very stressful for students as they stand in front of their peers and 'perform', with their pronunciation often suffering significantly due to nerves. But pronunciation-focused assessment can look and feel very different from this. It doesn't have to have an audience and it doesn't need to instil fear or anxiety. Instead, it can be a learner-centred experience that gives students personalized feedback on the intelligibility of their pronunciation of English and guidance on where to improve.

Why should we assess pronunciation?

A pronunciation test can allow you to identify your students' strengths and weaknesses, and to plan and personalize lesson content around any problematic features. This is sometimes referred to as a diagnostic test, and the problems it identifies can be addressed as they appear naturally in your teaching materials or in our students' own mispronunciations over time. We can also use assessment to measure our students' ability to use features of pronunciation taught in recent lessons or over a course of study. This is **progress testing**; using it can give students the sort of constructive feedback, guidance, or praise that will help them to feel more confident in their pronunciation. Finally, an achievement test allows us to measure a learner's level at the end of a course, term, or year.

What to test in a pronunciation assessment

Today, there are very few occasions where a student will need to replicate native-like English pronunciation in order to be understood, particularly if they are living, studying, and working in an international setting. As such, when selecting the pronunciation features to teach in the classroom and, in turn, to assess, consideration should first be given to those that will ensure intelligibility. One way of doing this is to incorporate the features from the Lingua Franca Core (see Chapter 1 and Appendix 1) into assessment, with a focus on most of the consonant sounds, consonant clusters, vowel-length contrasts, and the use of tonic stress.

Diagnostic tests

Try this    **Creating a read-aloud diagnostic test**

In this diagnostic test, students record themselves reading aloud a paragraph or set of sentences, and then submit the recording to you for assessment and feedback.

- Decide which feature(s) you wish to assess. To help you choose, keep in mind pronunciation features of the Lingua Franca Core (see Appendix 1).
- Find or create a suitable paragraph, or prepare a set of sentences for your students to read aloud, individually or in pairs. Students working individually could read a monologue from their coursebook, such as a radio news item. Students working in pairs could prepare a dialogue specific to their learning goals, such as a conversation with a doctor, a work colleague, or a customer. In both cases, ensure that the language is familiar; if it is too challenging, students could pay more attention to meaning, vocabulary, or grammar than to pronunciation.
- Whatever their origin, the texts to be recorded should include various instances of each feature to be assessed.

✓ Getting it right

Encourage your students to read and practise the paragraph or sentences as many times as they wish before submission. Provide clear instructions on how they should record the audio file and submit it to you. Recording options include:

- using a hand-held recording device;
- using a website such as Vocaroo or Flip onto which speech is directly recorded and a link sent to the teacher;
- recording directly onto a computer and sharing the mp3 file with you via a link to their own Google Drive or Dropbox;
- creating a recording through a recording app on their mobile phone, which is emailed to you or added to a shared drive such as Google Drive or Dropbox.

- Use a score sheet such as that shown in Figure 10.1 to provide feedback once the recordings have been submitted. A tick or a cross in the third column next to each word is a simple way to let students know if they have produced a feature intelligibly or not, and which specific words and features they need to improve.

Student name:			
Date:			
Feature	Word	✓ or ✗	Further feedback
/st/ **cluster**	stars start stop storm		
/sp/ **cluster**	space speed spin speak		
/p/	planets pioneer Pluto polar		
/b/	black hole Big Bang Theory billions background		

FIGURE 10.1. *Part of a score sheet used to mark students' diagnostic recordings based on a text about space and astronomy*

Why this works ⫸

Using a script for a diagnostic read-aloud test has a clear advantage: students cannot change the wording to avoid having to pronounce challenging sounds or other features. In addition, the feedback that the score sheet provides can raise students' awareness of mispronunciations they may not have been aware they were making. This awareness, together with their knowledge of what they have got right, can motivate them to improve.

One drawback of this format, however, is that students who struggle with reading and those with dyslexia may find that their problems with the written text prevent them from being able to provide you with an accurate sample of their pronunciation. To overcome this issue, use an additional task linked to the theme of the read-aloud script, such as a question they must respond to, or an image they must describe, with no need to read.

Assessing students' perception

When learners mispronounce something, it is not always a problem of production. Instead, it can come from their inability to perceive certain features. This is often the case with sentence stress and its tonic (the most emphasized word of a phrase or sentence; see Chapter 4). A simple diagnostic test of perception can help teachers to determine if the cause of a mispronunciation is a problem of production or one of perception.

Try this ☞   **Creating an in-class test to assess perception of tonic stress**

- Prepare a list of ten sentences. Write each one twice. Name the first sentence in each pair A and the second sentence in each pair B.
- In each pair of sentences, choose a different tonic, writing it in capital letters and bold, as shown in Figure 10.2.
- Give students a copy of the list and explain that in each sentence, the most stressed word is in capital letters and bold. They must listen to you as you read the sentences aloud and decide which one they hear you say: A or B.
- Give everyone a couple of minutes to read through the sentences for meaning, providing help as necessary.
- Read out either the A or the B version of the example sentence shown in Figure 10.2 to allow students to practise listening for the tonic before the assessment begins.
- Next, read through the test sentences, leaving a few moments between each for students to make their selection. Clearly emphasize the tonic syllable in each.
- Once you have finished reading out the sentences, go through the answers with the class, instructing them to mark their own test or a partner's.
- Collect the tests and look at the scores. If they got 60% or less correct, they would benefit from in-class activities to practise identifying tonic stress.

Listen to your teacher as they read
sentences 1–10. Pay attention to the
stressed word in capital letters
and bold. Do you hear sentence A or B?
Circle the sentence you hear.

Example sentence:

A. Did you go **HOME** for the holidays?

B. Did you go home for the **HOLIDAYS**?

1.

A. He's very angry **NOW**.

B. He's **VERY** angry now.

2.

A. He **DIDN'T** do the homework.

B. **HE** didn't do the homework.

3.

A. Do you **LIKE** the new teacher?

B. Do you like the **NEW** teacher?

4.

A. Would you like some **COFFEE**?

B. Would **YOU** like some coffee?

FIGURE 10.2.   *Part of a perception test to assess perception of tonic stress*

Why this works ▷

Many students carry over the sentence stress patterns of their mother tongue into English, unaware of how it affects their intelligibility. A diagnostic perception test allows both you and your students to see if this is an issue which affects them, and to plan upcoming lessons to practise identifying tonic stress. Alternatively, if students are scoring highly, turn your attention to their ability to produce stress to create meaning, as this has a significant impact on their intelligibility.

Progress tests

Try this ☞ **Creating a progress test**

An effective way to find out if students have absorbed recent instruction is through a progress test. This can be done in the middle or at the end of the course. If you use it mid-course, the results allow you to decide whether you need to recycle certain features. If you use it at the end of a course, this test allows us to make a final assessment of each student's ability to pronounce the features taught throughout the year.

- For a mid-course progress test, begin by reviewing the pronunciation features recently covered in class, and select those you would like to test. For an end-of-course test, take a selection from those you have taught throughout the course.
- Once you have chosen the pronunciation feature(s) you wish to test, create a range of activities for students to pronounce, all of which contain the target sounds or features. These could include:
  - ◆ eight minimal pair words (e.g. bat / pat);
  - ◆ four minimal pair sentences; for example:
    - Is that a **pea / bee**?
    - They really like **peaches / beaches**.
    - She said **bye / pie**.
    - I saw a **bear / pear**.
  - ◆ four sentences which require the student to change the most stressed word, i.e. the tonic stress; for example:
    - I took the bus to work
    - I took the bus to work
    - I took the bus to work.
    - I took the bus to work.
  - ◆ a read-aloud paragraph, or a dialogue recorded with a classmate.
- Provide students with a copy of the test and invite them to practise each item with a classmate and give each other feedback on how intelligible they sound.
- Tell the students to make their recordings at home. Explain that they can practise as many times as they like at home before making their recording and submitting it to you. Instruct them to start their recording by stating their name, the date, and their class details (e.g. Group 2H).
- As for the diagnostic test, prepare a score sheet to assess each student. However, this time, as you are marking, award a point for each item that is pronounced intelligibly. Once you have finished, add a final score, make some comments with constructive feedback, and praise as appropriate.

Why this works ⫸

Progress tests can keep students focused on their pronunciation throughout a course. They can also encourage students to revisit previous classes, review any teacher feedback, and listen to past recordings in the hope of improving their pronunciation.

Another benefit of progress tests that take the form of recordings is that students do not have to perform their assessment in front of the teacher or their peers. Instead, the recording is done at home, and shared only with one or two trusted classmates (for peer feedback) and their teacher. This can be especially welcome among teenage learners, or indeed in any class where students want to save face and avoid making mistakes in front of each other.

Using visuals to elicit speech in pronunciation assessments

Reading a scripted text aloud is not the only way to test students' pronunciation. Spontaneous speech is another good option, and images can be used as an effective way to elicit this. Using images in this way enables you to assess students without their needing to read anything.

Try this ☞   **Assessing pronunciation through image description**

In this activity, the teacher creates an image containing the pronunciation features to be tested. Students can work individually or with a partner to compare two slightly different images in a spot-the-difference activity.

- Decide which pronunciation features you would like to assess, and note down any objects or themes which would provoke the use of these features.
- Source royalty-free images of these items using websites such as Pixabay, Pexels, or the Noun Project. (The latter requires a user account.)
- Once you have found and downloaded the images you want to use, arrange them into a recognizable scene, such as a shopping street, a beach, a park, or a classroom, as shown in Figure 10.3. The items can be arranged on a PowerPoint slide, a Word document, or any online interactive whiteboard.
- Duplicate the image and then change half of the items in the second picture, ensuring they will still elicit the pronunciation features you want to assess. Figure 10.3, for example, contains twelve items per picture, all beginning with either /p/ or /b/.
  - ♦ Four items are the same in both pictures: books, a board, pens, and paper.
  - ♦ Items in Picture 1 testing /p/ are a pig, paints, a pink bag, and a plane. Items testing /b/ are a brown bag, boots, a basketball, and a bee.
  - ♦ Items in Picture 2 testing /p/ are a pear, plants, a present, and a pencil. Items testing /b/ are a bottle, a banana, a blue bird, and a basket.
- If you are testing students individually, ask them to begin by describing everything they see in Picture 1. They should then look carefully at Picture 2 and describe all the differences they see.
- If testing students in pairs, turn the simple spot-the-difference task into a Diapix activity. Diapix is a problem-solving task where students work in pairs, and each student receives only one of the spot-the-difference images. Without looking at

each other's image, they describe what they see and work together to identify all the differences. If the images in Figure 10.3 were used for a Diapix task, the students' conversation might sound something like this:

A: In my picture, there's a picture of a pig on the wall.
B: In mine, there's a picture of a pear.

B: I can see a bird from the window.
A: I can see a plane from the window.

FIGURE 10.3. *A spot-the-difference task made by arranging royalty-free images onto PowerPoint slides*

Diapix tasks are a useful way to measure students' pronunciation, and also provide you with an opportunity to assess their ability to use sentence stress, as the task requires them to emphasize what is different in their picture compared with their partner's, e.g. *In mine, there's a picture of a pear.* If you don't have time to create a scene, use one of the ready-made spot-the-difference or Diapix tasks available online.

✓ *Getting it right*

As with previous activities, this test can be recorded and submitted to you electronically for assessment. However, if done live, it gives you the option to help. For example, if students aren't producing the target features, you can elicit these by pointing at specific objects and asking *What can you see here?* or *What colour is this?*

Ensure that the images you select for this assessment are recognizable and appropriate for students' language level and learning context. Royalty-free images should provide you with enough content to make a test that is personalized to your students without having to worry about copyright.

Pair work assessment tasks

Pair work activities, such as role plays and dialogues, are an excellent way to elicit language for assessment using real-life scenarios. They can be based on topics and themes relating to students' lives beyond the classroom, and contain words and pronunciation features that can be re-used in a variety of different settings.

Try this ☞   **Assessing students' pronunciation using a semi-structured dialogue**

In this activity, students are given a real-life scenario which they must respond to by creating a dialogue with their partner.

- Provide students with a scenario appropriate to their learning context or goals, for example, asking for directions, requesting some time off work, providing an explanation, giving some advice.
- Give the students a vocabulary bank containing words that they should use in their dialogue, and which contain the pronunciation features you want to assess.
- Ask them to write a ten-line dialogue based on the scenario you have given them. Explain that the dialogue must contain:
  - ♦ a question;
  - ♦ a misunderstanding;
  - ♦ a correction;
  - ♦ a list of items;
  - ♦ at least two words from the vocabulary bank on every line of their dialogue.
- Give students a deadline by which they should have written, practised, recorded, and submitted the recording of their dialogue.

Why this works ⟩⟩⟩

> The real-life nature of these scenarios can make them more meaningful to students, who can draw inspiration from their own experiences to help them script their dialogue. The dialogue format works well as a final achievement test as it is flexible enough for you to use with as many or as few of the pronunciation features from a course as you wish. In addition, because the instructions detail the number of features to be included in each dialogue, each intelligibly pronounced item can be awarded with a mark, and so a final score can be given.

Monitoring students' progress and final achievement using portfolios

An excellent way of bringing together all of our students' pronunciation work during a course is to get them to keep a portfolio. This usually comes in the form of a digital online folder that teachers, classmates, and even interested family members can access. Student portfolios can be stored in a Google Drive, Dropbox, or Microsoft OneDrive folder, or in any similar cloud storage facility. A typical portfolio might contain:

1. the student's diagnostic test from the beginning of the course, along with the score sheet and any teacher feedback;
2. a recording of a list of words that the student struggles to produce;
3. a recording from any progress tests held midway through the course, plus the score sheets and teacher's feedback;
4. an audio or video recording where the student tells a story about a pronunciation mistake they made which resulted in a communication breakdown. The recording should document what happened, why it happened, and reflect on what the student could do to stop the same mistake happening again;

5. the script and recording of a short dialogue from the class coursebook – one that involves two people using sentence stress to clarify a misunderstanding;

6. a recording of an international sporting, music, or cinema celebrity speaking in English. The celebrity should have the same mother tongue as the student, who should record a brief audio note explaining why the celebrity inspires them;

7. a recording of an achievement test held in the final stages of the course, including the score sheet and teacher feedback;

8. an audio or video reflection made by the student at the end of the course which documents;
   - their experience using the pronunciation portfolio;
   - the features they have improved and those that still needed more practice;
   - any changes in their confidence when speaking;
   - their pronunciation goals for the future.

APPENDICES

Appendix 1: The Lingua Franca Core (LFC)

In the 1990s, language experts became aware that non-native speakers were using English successfully for international communication in ways that did not always conform to native-speaker use. This raised the question as to what exact form this non-native-speaker English might take, and researchers set about the task of trying to codify it. Jennifer Jenkins pioneered the research in the area of pronunciation, and her data allowed her to determine that four aspects of pronunciation were central to international intelligibility in EIL contexts. These four aspects make up what Jenkins termed the Lingua Franca Core (see Chapter 1).

LFC feature	Examples and comments
Most consonant sounds	The correct pronunciation of most consonant sounds is a key feature of the LFC. The pronunciation of /f/ as /p/, for example, with *coffee* sounding like *copy*, could seriously impair international intelligibility. Similarly, replacing /n/ with /l/ would make *next* or *nose* into nonsense words, which would be virtually impossible to understand, even in clear contexts.
	Exceptions: There are widely intelligible variations to three consonants: /θ/, /ð/, and /r/. The /θ/ in *think* can be pronounced as /t/, /f/ or /s/ (i.e. as 'tink', 'fink', or 'sink') and still be perfectly intelligible. Similarly, the /ð/ in *then* can be pronounced as /d/ or /z/ (i.e. as 'den' or 'zen'), and remain intelligible. Finally, the /r/ in *ready* can be pronounced as a trilled *r* without any loss of intelligibility.
Other consonant sounds: aspiration of /p/, /t/, and /k/	A lack of aspiration of the consonant sounds /p/, /t/, and /k/ at the beginning of a word or stressed syllable threatens intelligibility. The sound /p/ can be mistaken for /b/, the sound /t/ for /d/, and the sound /k/ for /g/. For example, *pear* can sound like *bear*, *tip* like *dip*, and *coat* like *goat*.
Consonant clusters	Consonant clusters (i.e. two or more consonants together) are another key LFC feature. Speakers from some languages often simplify the clusters in English, either by deleting one of the consonants, or by inserting a weak vowel between two consonants. Of these two strategies, adding a vowel is much less damaging to intelligibility than deleting a consonant. Thus, while the pronunciation of *sting* as 'esting' or *stone* as 'sitone' is not found to threaten intelligibility, the deletion of one of the consonants does, since it produces either 'sing', or the nonsense word 'ting', which might be understood as 'thing'. Employing the correct strategy is especially important for clusters at the beginning or in the middle of words.

Vowel sounds

The vowels of English can be described in terms of their quality and their length. Quality refers to the differences in the way speakers from different English-speaking countries or from different regions of the same country pronounce a vowel. The *u* in the word *bus*, for example, is pronounced differently by speakers from SE England, the Midlands, or NE England, and is part of each region's local accent. Vowel quality is not fundamental for international intelligibility. The variation in vowel quality that individual speakers make will be intelligible providing they are consistent in their own particular way of pronouncing the different vowels of English.

In contrast, the length distinction between long and short vowels such as in *feel* and *fill*, is a core feature. This same length characteristic extends to diphthongs, which are about the same length as the long vowels. In addition, there is a marked shortening of the length of all English vowels (pure vowels and diphthongs) when they come before voiceless consonants. This characteristic means that the long vowel /iː/, for example, is shorter in *seat* than in *seed*, that the vowel /æ/ is shorter in *back* than in *bag*, or that the diphthong /eɪ/ is shorter in *mate* than in *maid*. This shortening effect is known as pre-fortis clipping, and is key to intelligibility.

Sentence stress

Sentence stress (also known as tonic stress or nuclear stress) refers to the existence of stressed and unstressed syllables in a phrase or sentence. English deliberately stresses one word or syllable in each phrase or sentence more than the others. The choice of stressed syllable can give a sentence a specific meaning. 'When did you GET here?' doesn't have the same meaning as 'When did YOU get here?' or 'When did you get HERE?'. The words are the same, but the different choice of most stressed syllable has changed, and that changes the meaning of the question.

In addition, the most stressed syllable inevitably becomes the focus of the listener's attention. Because of this, placing the tonic stress in the wrong place can seriously affect how the listener processes entire chunks of speech. Correct sentence stress, then, is key to international intelligibility.

Word stress

Word stress was not included in the original LFC. It was considered to be a grey area that might or might not be important. However, in the absence of clear evidence to indicate the positive or negative impact of word stress on international intelligibility, it is best to include it in our list of teaching priorities. Apart from the fact that future evidence may show word stress to be important, it can be a useful pedagogical tool when you are trying to introduce sentence stress.

A number of features of the pronunciation of English lie outside the Lingua Franca Core, and are not necessary for international intelligibility. These non-LFC features include the consonant known as dark 'l', exact vowel quality (see above), tones (i.e. the up and down movement of the pitch of the voice), stress-timing (i.e. the rhythm of English), weak forms, schwa, and some connected speech features.

Not only are non-core features such as dark 'l', vowel quality, tones, and stress-timed rhythm difficult for learners to master, but their presence or absence has little or no impact on international intelligibility. At best, they might be considered low priority for certain learners. Schwa and weak forms are also difficult to master. More importantly, these features, though typical of native-speaker pronunciation, can actually make speakers less internationally intelligible. This is because they reduce syllables to such an extent that whole syllables may disappear from speech. The disappearance of syllables can completely alter how a word is heard. The word *particularly*, for example, can sound more like /pˈtɪkli/. Being able to understand English spoken in this way can be helpful for learners who will have regular dealings with native speakers, but being able to produce these reductions does not help speakers to be internationally intelligible. These non-LFC features, then, are characteristics of English pronunciation that learners need to be able to understand, but shouldn't be encouraged to learn to produce.

Appendix 2: Glossary

Accent The result of differences in pronunciation between speakers. Accents can be regional or social. English as an International Language (EIL) sees learners' accents and the accents of native speakers as equally valid.

Accommodation The ability to adjust your speech and other aspects of spoken communication so that they become more like that of your interlocutors. Accommodation can be productive (i.e. adjustments are made while speaking), or receptive (i.e. adjustments are made while listening).

Articulators The movable parts of the mouth that are used to make different sounds: the sounds of English are made using the lips, the teeth, the tongue, and the jaw.

Aspiration A small puff of air that immediately follows the consonants /p/, /t/, /k/ when they are at the beginning of a stressed syllable in English. The word *take*, for example, could be transcribed as [tʰeɪk] to show that the first /t/ is aspirated.

CAPT (Computer-assisted pronunciation teaching) The use of computer software or apps to provide learners with guidance and practice in pronunciation, often in the absence of a physical teacher and outside the classroom.

Connected speech The way that individual words come together in short bursts of sound with no audible gaps between words. Connected speech often produces changes in the pronunciation of individual sounds or whole words, creating problems of understanding for listeners who are used to hearing words in isolation.

Consonant cluster A group of two or more consonants that come together in an individual word, or when two words come together. The word *consonants* has two clusters: 'ns' and 'nts'. The phrase *last drop* has a four-consonant cluster: 'stdr'.

Content word A noun, verb, adjective, or adverb that carries the key idea in a message.

English as an International Language (EIL) English taught to non-native speakers so that they can communicate principally with other non-native speakers. This is very similar to English as a Lingua Franca.

General American (GA) An accent that is often referred to as the norm when teaching American English pronunciation. It is felt to lack any of the characteristics of US regional or ethnic accents.

Intelligibility The extent to which the words a speaker says are understood by the listener. A common test of intelligibility is to transcribe what the speaker says. Listeners will be able to transcribe 100% of the words spoken by a fully intelligible speaker.

International intelligibility The ability to speak English in a way that is intelligible to listeners from all around the world who use English for international communication. The majority of these listeners will be non-native speakers. Native speakers are not automatically internationally intelligible.

Lexical stress See **Word stress**.

Lingua Franca Core (LFC) A small set of pronunciation features that the analysis of fieldwork data has shown to be central to international intelligibility (see Appendix 1).

Minimal pair Two words that differ in pronunciation by only one sound, such as *bat* and *hat*, *her* and *here*, or *make* and *made*.

Nuclear stress See **Sentence stress**.

Phonics A method of teaching reading by matching the letters and letter combinations that make up words to different spoken sounds. For example, the letters 'ee' in *seen* or *been* are pronounced /iː/, and the letters 'ght' in *night* are pronounced /t/.

Progress testing Assessment carried out during a course of study in order to see if the learners have improved in specific areas taught over the more recent part of the course.

Received Pronunciation (RP) An accent that until now has been used as the norm when teaching British English pronunciation. It is a minority accent in the UK but is often viewed as being the correct accent for teaching purposes.

Schwa The weak vowel sound /ə/ that is only found in unstressed syllables in spoken English, e.g. in the 'or' of *doctor* or the first 'a' in *again*.

Sentence stress In a spoken phrase or sentence, only certain words are stressed (normally nouns, verbs, adjectives, and adverbs), and one word is stressed more than the others. Sentence stress is the way this most stressed word creates specific meanings. For example, *They're arriving on Friday* has a different meaning from *They're arriving on Friday*. Also called **nuclear stress**.

Unvoiced See **Voicing**.

Voicing The use (or not) of the vocal cords in making certain consonant sounds. Sounds that are made with vibration in the vocal cords are known as 'voiced'. When the vocal cords do not vibrate, a sound is 'unvoiced (or 'voiceless'). The sounds /p/ and /b/ differ only in voicing: /b/ is voiced and /p/ is unvoiced.

Vowel weakening In colloquial native-speaker speech, unstressed vowels are often pronounced with significantly less effort and volume. This weakening of the vowels can cause them to change their pronunciation, usually to schwa. This is the case with the unstressed vowel in 'doctor', for example (/ˈdɒktə(r)/), or with the vowels in the first and third syllables in 'computer' (/kəmˈpjuːtə(r)/).

Weak form Some grammatical classes of words such as preposition, conjunctions, pronouns, or auxiliary verbs have a strong form pronunciation when they are stressed, and a weak form pronunciation when they are unstressed. The most common vowel in weak forms is schwa.

Word stress In words of more than one syllable, some syllables are produced with greater force and loudness than others. These strong syllables are fixed for a given word. The word stress in *often* is on the first syllable, while for *begin*, it is on the second.

Appendix 3:
Recommended reading

English pronunciation for a global world [PDF]

Walker, R., Low, E., & Setter, J. (2021). Oxford University Press.
The OUP Position Paper on pronunciation. The authors of the paper provide expert advice and evidence-based guidance as to the why, what, and how of an international intelligibility (EIL) approach to teaching pronunciation. Download for free at https://elt.oup.com/feature/global/expert/.

Teaching the pronunciation of English as a Lingua Franca

Walker, R. (2010). Oxford University Press.
The only teacher's handbook to explore the benefits of taking an international intelligibility approach to teaching pronunciation. There are specific chapters on the Lingua Franca Core, the benefits and challenges of an EIL approach, classroom techniques, using the learner's L1, and planning and assessment. More information at https://elt.oup.com/catalogue/.

Mark Hancock's 50 tips for pronunciation teaching

Hancock, M. (2020). Cambridge University Press.
50 very practical tips that cover three important areas of pronunciation teaching: goals and models, what to teach, and how to teach it. The tips are aimed at classroom teachers and have a clear orientation towards teaching pronunciation for intelligibility.

Teaching American English pronunciation

Avery, P., & Ehrlich, S. (1992). Oxford University Press.
Written specifically for language teachers, this OUP handbook gives a clear description of English consonants and vowels for North American English, together with practical ideas for dealing with common pronunciation problems.

Appendix 4: Useful websites

AccentBase https://www.youtube.com/@AccentBase

A mapping of the accents of the English-speaking world. Most of the accents are those of native speakers, but PLAYLISTS on the menu bar, and then 'Second Language', leads to recordings with non-native speakers. Useful for Chapters 6, 7, and 8.

Canva http://www.canva.com

An online design platform which, with a free user account, provides access to a number of creative tools, as well as online interactive whiteboards. Useful for Chapters 3 and 10.

Diapix https://www.ucl.ac.uk/pals/research/speech-hearing-and-phonetic-sciences/shaps-research/diapix

A type of spot-the-difference task that can be used to elicit spontaneous speech between two participants. The participants have to try and work out the differences between their pictures without seeing their partner's. Useful for Chapter 10.

Dynamic Dialects www.dynamicdialects.ac.uk

Using an accent map and accent chart, users can listen to vowel sounds pronounced by speakers from countries where English is a first or second language. Useful for Chapter 8.

EnglishGlobalCommunication https://englishglobalcom.wordpress.com

Robin Walker's website, with numerous articles for free download on pronunciation teaching for international intelligibility. The blog *An A–Z of Pronunciation* covers many of the issues raised in this book. The final post, *Z – the end of the road*, has an alphabetical list of all of the topics explored in the blog. Useful for all chapters.

ELLLO (English Listening Library Online) https://elllo.org/

Over 1500 audio and 700 video recordings of native and non-native speakers, teachers, and students talking about a huge range of topics. The recordings come with a transcript that you can show or hide at will. Useful for Chapters 6, 7, and 8.

Flip https://info.flip.com

A free app from Microsoft that allows teachers to create online groups for students to express their ideas in short video and audio messages. Useful for Chapter 10.

Hancock MacDonald http://hancockmcdonald.com

The website of Mark Hancock and Annie MacDonald, who are ELT authors, teachers, and trainers. The site offers abundant free classroom materials and downloads for both pronunciation teaching and listening skills. Useful for Chapters 2, 3, 4, 9, and 10.

International Dialects of English Archive https://www.dialectsarchive.com/

More than 1,600 recordings, where each speaker reads a scripted text and then speaks spontaneously. The *Special Collections* section offers two sets of listening comprehension activities – *Test Your Ear* and *Test Your Comprehension*. Useful for Chapters 6, 7, and 8.

My English Voice https://www.youtube.com/@myenglishvoice192

This site is specifically for students aiming at international intelligibility. It offers a small number of interesting videos of mainly non-native speakers talking about themselves and their use of English. Useful for Chapters 1 and 6.

Pexels https://www.pexels.com

Royalty-free images and videos that can be downloaded and used free. Useful for Chapter 10.

Pixabay https://pixabay.com

Royalty-free images that can be used for language testing. Useful for Chapter 10.

Rev Recorder https://www.rev.com/onlinevoicerecorder

An online recording and transcription service that also offers a free voice-recorder app for iPhone and Android. This is easy to use and gives a simple waveform for each recording. Useful for Chapter 4.

The Speech Accent Archive https://accent.gmu.edu/

Over 3,000 samples of native and non-native speakers of English, all reading the same paragraph. Select 'browse' from the menu on the home page, and then 'language/speakers' to access the recordings by accent. Useful for Chapters 6, 7, and 8.

Vocaroo https://vocaroo.com

Vocaroo is a simple, free audio-recording tool which works in the web browser of computers and mobile devices. Users can easily share their recordings via email, QR code, or social media. Useful for Chapters 6 and 10.

Wavepad https://www.nch.com.au/wavepad/index.html

Wavepad is professional audio-editing software but there is an app for iPhone and Android. It is more complete than Rev Recorder, but a little less easy to use as a result. Useful for Chapters 6 and 10.

YouGlish https://youglish.com

More than 100 million video tracks of principally native speakers. You can search the tracks to find a word or phrase, and follow the recording with the aid of the transcription. You can replay the word/phrase as often as you need, at varying speeds. Useful for Chapter 8.